W9-CMZ-720

Hollow

an unpolished tale

jena morrow

Hollow, a memoir by Jena Marrow, shares the honest truth of human brokenness. Her life's journey is like that of so many; and anyone walking the path of redemptive growth will be enlightened and guided by Jena's vulnerability. As a clinical psychologist, I know it is through gracious relationship that people are healed; *Hollow* evokes a sincere, healing relationship between the reader and Jena's story of grace.

—R. Allen Lish, PsyD

Jena offers hope to those struggling with an eating disorder, or to those just wondering if what they have to offer is good. Her authentic and courageous telling of her journey thus far is a true testimony to the goodness of God in the midst of our struggles.

—Kris Walsh, LCSW

This is no graphic drama told for entertainment purposes. In Jena's words, it is a "cautionary tale" told by one who tarried in the darkness, but who no longer lives there. Jena's story moves beyond the slippery darkness into the strength of relationship with the Living God, and she is eager to invite along many companions.

—Jill Fleagle, DMin

As a family nurse practitioner, this is a memoir that has made me a better health care provider by enabling me to recognize those struggling and get them the help they need before they reach such depths of darkness. *Hollow* reaches out to all people who struggle in life, and guides the reader to the power of God in helping with these struggles. This book is an awakening.

—Linda Silakowski, FNP

If you or a loved one needs to know there really is a way out of the strong clutches of the self-hatred of an eating disorder, you will want to walk with Jena through each page. You will find a new strength and a fresh hope.

—Gregory L. Jantz, PhD, C.E.D.S.
Founder, The Center, Inc.

Hollow pulled me into a world I knew little about, held me there with its raw authenticity, and gave me empathy for those who struggle with eating disorders. Anyone battling food issues should read this book. But more than that, anyone who loves someone in an eating disorder's clutches should scour its pages for understanding.

—Mary DeMuth
Author of *Thin Places, a Memoir*

Too often we want the fairytale ending. In *Hollow: An Unpolished Tale*, new author Jena Morrow treats us to an uncommonly honest portrayal of the recovery journey, and makes a hope-filled case for facing our fears, embracing our anger, and surrendering to the only One who can calm the storm within—even if (and when) it continues to rage.

—Constance Rhodes
Founder, FINDINGbalance,
Cofounder, The True Campaign

Not just a haunting tale of a wicked disorder, but the story of a tenacious God who does not give up on His children. Jena's story offers reality and hope to the millions of people (not counting their relatives and friends) impacted by eating disorders.

—Jane Rubietta
Speaker and award-winning author
of critically acclaimed *Come Along:
The Journey to a More Intimate Faith*

HOLLOW

An Unpolished Tale

Jena Morrow

MOODY PUBLISHERS

CHICAGO

© 2010 by
JENA MORROW

All Scripture quotations, unless otherwise indicated, are taken from the *Holy Bible, New International Version*®, NIV®. Copyright © 1973, 1978, 1984 by Biblica, Inc.™ Used by permission of Zondervan.
All rights reserved worldwide.

Scripture quotations marked NLT are taken from the *Holy Bible, New Living Translation*, copyright © 1996, 2004. Used by permission of Tyndale House Publishers, Inc., Wheaton Illinois 60189, U.S.A. All rights reserved.

Scripture quotations marked NASB are taken from the *New American Standard Bible*®, Copyright © 1960, 1962, 1963, 1968, 1971, 1972, 1973, 1975, 1977, 1995 by The Lockman Foundation. Used by permission. (www.Lockman.org)

To protect the privacy of fellow patients, friends, and professionals, pseudonyms are used in place of their real names.

Editor: Annette LaPlaca
Interior Design: Julia Ryan / DesignByJulia.com
Cover Design: Tan Nguyen
Cover Image: PJZ Studios

Library of Congress Cataloging-in-Publication Data

Morrow, Jena.
  Hollow : an unpolished tale / Jena Morrow.
    p. cm.
  Includes bibliographical references.
  ISBN 978-0-8024-4871-2
1. Morrow, Jena. 2. Anorexia nervosa--Patients--Religious life.
3. Anorexia nervosa--Religious aspects--Christianity. I. Title.
  BV4910.35.M67 2010
  248.8'625092--dc22
  [B]

                        2009053306

This book is printed on acid free recycled paper containing 30% PCW (Post Consumer Waste) and manufactured in the United States of America by Bethany Press.

We hope you enjoy this book from Moody Publishers. Our goal is to provide high-quality, thought-provoking books and products that connect truth to your real needs and challenges. For more information on other books and products written and produced from a biblical perspective, go to www.moodypublishers.com or write to:

Moody Publishers
820 N. LaSalle Boulevard
Chicago, IL 60610

1 3 5 7 9 10 8 6 4 2

Printed in the United States of America

In loving memory of
My dear friend Cindy
1975–2005

CONTENTS

Acknowledgments
Foreword: Jill Sidler Fleagle, D.Min, LPC
Prologue: Life as I Know It

1	Liar, Liar	20
2	A Defective Model	26
3	Choose Whom You Will Serve	34
4	Disappearing Act	41
5	Little Girl on Campus	53
6	At Any Cost	65
7	Pull Up a Couch	71
8	Wading Deeper	78
9	In Meg We Trust	87
10	When God Closes A Door	94
11	Bon Voyage	101
12	Welcome to Wonderland	106
13	Newbies	116
14	Off to a Rough Start	125
15	Paying through the Nose	131
16	Digging In	138
17	All in the Family	144
18	God Whispers	149
19	Life on the Inside	161
20	The Art of Being	168
21	Changing of the Guard	178
22	The Agony of Victory	190
23	Halfway to Somewhere	198
24	Ashes, Ashes, We All Fall Down	212
25	And the Beat Goes On	218
26	A Work in Progress	228
27	Can We Talk?	232

Epilogue: Choosing the Way 236

FOREWORD

I met Jena when she came to my home for some quiet time set apart to meet with Lord Jesus. Jena is beautiful to behold. I did not know her story then, but I believed her arrival to be a God-appointment I eagerly anticipated. I hoped to be a vessel of ministry in her life. Indeed, as I have grown to know in part her inner beauty, depth, and spunk, I have become the grateful recipient of Jena.

In these pages, Jena takes readers to an anything-but-glamorous place most would never freely choose to go. This agonizingly gripping travelogue of a journey into a kind of hell on earth is a story that must be told. While this is Jena's story, hers is not a solitary journey. Current statistics cite 8 million Americans who suffer from eating disorders, one in every 200 struggling with anorexia nervosa. Sometimes it's necessary to face the dark, haunting places before one comes to live freely in the light. Jena journeys from haunting to hope—a hope she holds out to any who would dare to believe in the possibility that life can be chosen one day at a time.

This is no graphic drama told for entertainment purposes. In Jena's words, it is a "cautionary tale" told by one who tarried in the darkness, but who no longer lives there. Jena's story moves beyond the slippery darkness into the strength of relationship with the living God. Just as her descent into anorexia was no solitary journey, so her wading into God's mercy requires journey companions. Jena came to know her place in the grandest of all love stories. It's the love story every one of us needs to hear, because it was written for each one of us.

Jill Sidler Fleagle, D.Min (candidate), LPC
Licensed Professional Counselor
Crossroads Counseling and Care Center
Crest Hill, Illinois

The cold, hard ceramic tiles are
a punishment to my protruding spine: a
row of golf balls down my back, pressed
against the bathroom floor, bruising. At
first, I do not know how I have come here,
eyes half-open, unseeing. From far away,
I hear muffled tones on the other side of
the door: *Thanks for coming so quickly this
time . . . probably fainted getting out of the tub
. . . she's anorexic . . . happened once before . . .*

I fight against the invisible arms that
hold me down. I try to back away from
the vanishing point toward which I've been
floating. *Got to wake up, got to wake up, got
to wake UP!* I cannot let them find me lying
on the floor naked, exposed for all to see.
I cannot let them see, or they will know:
I'm not so thin at all.

ANOREXIA NERVOSA:

A psychological illness, most common in female adolescents, in which the patients have no desire to eat; eating may, in fact, be abhorrent to them. The problem often starts with a simple desire to lose weight, which then becomes an obsession. The result is severe loss of weight and sometimes even death from starvation. The underlying cause of the illness is complicated— problems in the family and rejection of adult sexuality are often factors involved. Patients must usually be treated by psychotherapy.

Concise Medical Dictionary
(Oxford Medical Publications, Britain)

A psychological and endocrine disorder primarily of young women in their teens that is characterized especially by a pathological fear of weight gain leading to faulty eating patterns, malnutrition, and usually excessive weight loss.

Webster's Ninth New Collegiate Dictionary (USA)

Therefore we do not lose heart. Though outwardly we are wasting away, yet inwardly we are being renewed day by day.

2 Corinthians 4:16

Life As I Know It

f you are relatively normal, you probably wake up in the morning, rub your eyes and hit the snooze button, climb out of bed, put on your slippers and your robe, visit the bathroom on your way to the kitchen, where you switch on the coffeepot, pour some cereal or crack a couple of eggs into a pan, and then sit down with the morning paper and your breakfast. You don't just stare at your breakfast; you eat it. You do it almost without thinking. Around noon, you take a break from whatever you are doing—caring for children or selling cars or trading stocks—and eat again. And you eat again five or six hours later. Eating does not consume your thoughts; it is part of life. It is what you do, in fact, to *sustain* life.

If you are me, or one of millions like me, your day looks a bit different. There is sleep and there is work and there is life and there are children—and books and movies and play dates and girls' nights. And there is food. But the food is not eaten casually or carelessly or even comfortably. Rather it is weighed, measured, agonized over, feared, loved, hated, resented, desired. You do not understand the meaning of such casual phrases as "grab a bite" or "do lunch." You do not understand how people can joke about busting the buttons off of their jeans after a big meal, but you wish you could. You wish the idea of gaining a few pounds was a little inconvenience of life, about which you could shrug and say, "Guess I'll start my diet tomorrow." But the idea is terrifying, and the fact that it is so terrifying is embarrassing. But this is life as you know it, if you have an eating disorder.

There are good days, and better days, and horrible-awful-no-good-very-bad days. There was a time in my life when life itself stopped due to my disorder, and I became an invalid, a mental case dressed in a hospital gown and purple nail polish with perfectly applied makeup. This, thank God, is no longer the case. I have rejoined the ranks of the living, though some days I am tentative about the follow-through. The eating disorder is no longer my tyrannical puppeteer, but rather something of an evil twin, forever at my side, vying for dominance. She is not pleasant, but she has not killed me, and for this I must be thankful. For the most part, I bicker with her throughout the day, begging her to shut the heck up. I have a life to live, after all; I'm *busy*. I don't need her, don't have time for her or the craziness she brings, and I tell her so.

Life has become, incrementally, more appealing to me than death. Life offers me things that death does not, like birthday parties and road trips and Christmas dinners and dates and movie nights. Of course, there is a common thread among these things: food. And this detail still complicates things for me, especially once the evil twin wakes up beside me the morning after.

Cake? she says, meeting me in the bathroom mirror as I undress for the shower. *You ate cake last night? What were you thinking? I never gave you permission to eat cake. And now you'll pay for it, you greedy pig. Get on the scale. Now!*

"I don't want to," I say. "Please. I'm sorry; I won't let it happen again."

You bet you won't, she hisses. *You should be disgusted with yourself. Cake . . . Unbelievable. What an indulgent wretch.*

"It was a party," I reason. "My friends were over. We all had cake. I'm allowed to have a piece of cake with my friends!"

Shut up! she snaps. *Your friends are allowed cake. You are not. Now . . . you know what you need to do.*

"No," I say. "Please. Not today. I won't eat all day today; I promise."

You got that right, you spoiled, selfish cow, she seethes. *And you're gonna pay for yesterday. Open the cabinet.*

"No," I beg, silently. "I don't want to be sick today."

Take them, she orders.

"But—"

Take the pills, any you can find. Do it! I don't care what—just take something. You've been bad, and you must be punished.

"But I—"

Oh, stop it. You knew this would happen.

I open the cabinet. I stare at my stash of pills and syrups. They're where they always are. Not to use, I tell myself. Just to have on hand. Just in case.

Take them, Jena.

"I don't want to."

Take them now, Jena.

"I'm allowed to eat a piece of cake!"

You're a fat failure.

"I'm not a failure."

Look like one to me.

"Shut UP!"

(Laughter.) You have a big bottle of migraine pills. Take them all, and I'll leave you alone. I swear. (More laughter.)

I start to cry, weakening. I know that she is a liar, that she has no intention of leaving me alone, not even if I obey her commands to hurt myself. I know that she is a bully, and that my demise is all that concerns her. And still she tempts me, every time. I want what she promises, and she knows just which buttons to push. She is evil, and she is good at what she does.

I am not without my defenses. I know what to do. I've had years and years of counseling, which have prepared me for this battle. I have index cards, tucked away everywhere, all over my house. There are some in the kitchen, by the food. There are some in my closet, by my clothes. There is a good-sized stack of them here in the bathroom, by the mirror. They are my affirmations, carefully selected Scripture passages I am to read aloud in these particularly dicey moments, when I teeter on the edge, tempted to give in to this voice of sickness. I feel like an idiot when I have to pull them out and read them; I feel I should not need them at this stage in the game. The trouble is, it's a game I am certain to lose without the truth of God's Word. And so, feeling like an idiot, I grab the cards. Feeling like an idiot, I read them.

"I am God's creation, made in His image. God takes pleasure in me."

(*Uneasy silence.*)

"I am the righteousness of God in Christ. I have been chosen and set apart for God's holy purpose."

(*Nothing.*)

"I am not condemned, not by myself, not by God. I have a purpose to fulfill on this earth, and I will not hate myself. And I will not die today."

(*Silence.*)

"Do you hear me? I *will not* die today!"

The voice falls quiet. I've worn her down, and the Word of God has shut her up, for now. This little conversation is not unusual. It's not an audible voice, of course. The accusatory words are more like extremely loud thoughts that assert themselves against the saner, more reasonable part of my brain.

I close the medicine cabinet and slide down the bathroom wall, slumping onto the vinyl floor. I'm exhausted, tired of these silly arguments with myself. And I'm fat. She has convinced me of that much. But today, I do not back down. I do not take the pills or swallow the syrups. Today, by the grace of God and the truth of His Word, I win.

————————

My struggle may seem intense, and it certainly feels that way at times. But my plight is not unique or uncommon. We're American women, after all, and it seems we have been bred for this war against our weight. For some, the struggle is legitimate and physical, and our weight is a threat to our health, cosmetic and aesthetic concerns aside. For others, we sigh about the same pesky ten pounds that have clung like unwelcome houseguests for more years than we care to calculate. We play with those pounds—adding them, analyzing them, explaining them, excusing them: "I really need to drop this baby weight," we chastise ourselves as we glance at said baby, now entering first grade or ninth grade or grad school—but never have we done what we had planned to with good intentions: get 'em gone for good.

Modern women are sister soldiers in this battle, regardless of where the needle falls when we climb on that miniature stage that we call the scale. When the battleground is our hips or bottoms or bellies or thighs, we know the drill. The over-simplified mantra of "eat less, move more" has become a Pavlovian response we can recite on command when asked for our battle plan. It's not brain surgery, after all.

But what if the *brain* is the battleground? What if our hips and bottoms and bellies and thighs are only excessive in the mirror of our mind? And what if that mirror talks back, like the cocky smart-mouthed mirror in *Snow White,* and what if we can't get it to shut up?

My mirror is broken, metaphorically speaking, and my eyes cannot be trusted to tell me the truth. I live in a maze of fun-house mirrors, never quite sure which reflection is really me. I walk into a fitting room with the same jeans in five different sizes because I truly cannot estimate what size I wear. I am forever engaged in a silent battle in my head over whether or not to lift the fork to my mouth, and when I talk myself into taking the bite, I taste only shame.

The disease has been with me for nearly all of my life. It was the mean monster in my mind that convinced me I was fat when I was three years old. It was the tyrannical voice in my head hissing insults throughout the already-awkward years of adolescence and puberty, calling me fat and clumsy and stupid and inadequate. And it was the bully in my brain that turned on me when I was a teenager and forbade me to eat.

The disease has been a crutch, a companion, a coping mechanism, an excuse, a speed bump, a deceptive lover, an attractive abuser. It has made part of my life a roller coaster ride in and out of hospitals and treatment centers, day programs and sober living homes, the sum total of which adds up to several hundred thousand dollars in treatment costs. It has strained my friendships, derailed my career path, harmed my body, and bruised my soul.

Like any addict, I have spent years both on the wagon and off. I have been sick, sicker, hospitalized, better, almost well, sick again, in treatment, sicker, sicker yet, better, etc. I have met and befriended some amazing women—and a few young men— who share my struggle with eating disorders. They are the silver lining to a very gray disease. I have loved them, fought with them, watched some of them get better, get well, get married, have children. I have watched others get sick, get sicker still, and die.

When my friend Cindy died from her eating disorder in 2005, I decided the time had come to put words to the fight and release some of the emotions that for years had plagued me, which were stirred up by the tragically premature loss of a life. Since I was old enough to hold a pencil and form words, writing has always been my way of responding to a world that at once scares and overwhelms me, surprises and delights me.

I've heard it said that a writer should write what she knows. I know a little about a lot of things. I could write a few sentences about music, and maybe a paragraph about theater, and even an essay about being a single mother. I know a bit about living life as a ragamuffin lover of Jesus, and I know a few things about art and writing and letting one's creative inner child run wild. Someday I may learn more about these worlds of possibility so I might write on them and, grandiosely enough, contribute to the world. I'm sure it's that simple: do your research, and change the world. But eating disorders, unfortunately, I know. I've *lived* the research.

And, grandiosely enough, I want to take what I know and use it to affect at least my little corner of the world. I didn't live through this for nothing, and writing this book seemed a good way to prove it.

My story will not glamorize eating disorders, as many books do. It will not be a how-to guide for those wanting to jump on board the anorexia train. That train derails, every time. This is a cautionary tale, a little study on the darker side of human behavior, and a slice-of-life story about finding God in odd places—or, rather, about being found *by* God no matter how fast we try to run away from Him. It's a love story, of sorts.

The events and people involved have spanned the course of years and multiple facilities and groups. In the interest of making the story readable and easier to follow, I have consolidated some people and events. I also must disclose the fact that I was out of mind with mania and starvation and sleep deprivation when most of these events took place, and I have had to take some liberties to fill in the blank spaces between coherent memories. It is difficult to write a memoir about an eating disorder, because an eating disorder numbs the mind, shutting off the sufferer from her circumstances.

I've tried very hard to die over the course of my life, all the while under the impression that I was trying to *live*. I've flirted with death like young girls flirt with dirty old men on the Internet, never aware how real the danger was. I probably shouldn't be alive today. If we lived under a system of justice wherein we got what we deserved, I would have croaked years ago. But, thanks to an incredibly merciful and forgiving God and a body too hearty and stubborn to die, I'm here.

I didn't think I would make it to thirty-three. I had a hunch during my teen years that I would check out early, maybe by my midtwenties, and leave others standing around shaking their heads and saying, "Such a shame." It's a heady, self-serving fantasy, really.

But that fantasy didn't come true. I always seemed to get better in the nick of time, before my heart stopped or I stroked out or I found the resolve to take every pill in my medicine cabinet. Something always stopped me. Someone always spoke up or butted in or stormed out, bringing me to my senses—or at least to the dinner table. And I'm glad I made it here. "Here" is a pretty decent place to be, if not always comfortable. Because, while I still have an eating disorder (today it is classified as EDNOS, or Eating Disorder Not Otherwise Specified), a funny thing has happened: I have fallen out of love with it.

You've caught me on a good day. Things have happened over the past few years that God has used to screw my head on a little tighter. I am a mom. I am, for all intents and purposes, an adult. I have a house and a kid and a car and bills and cats. I have responsibilities, among them to advise others not to go where I went and tell those already there not to drop anchor in eating disorder territory.

It is my hope and my prayer that this book accomplishes that.

Liar, Liar

*O*ctober 1979. I am three years old. I sit beside my mother in the front seat of her silver Grand Prix, in the days long before child-seat laws, as we drive home from preschool. She is asking about my day, asking me to explain the crayon drawing I made of a turkey with rainbow feathers. I cannot answer her, though, because I am distracted by the way my legs squish themselves out wide as I sit back on the passenger seat, my black-and-white saddle shoes dangling ten inches above the floor mat, and the way the zipper of my pink windbreaker billows away from my body and makes me look like I have a baby in my belly.

And suddenly, it occurs to me that I am fat. Photos of me at age three show a snub-nosed, pigtailed, blonde toddler wearing green bell-bottoms and a wide silly grin, always with a baby doll tucked protectively under the arm. These photos also prove I was anything but fat. The terrible irony is that I have never actually *been* fat, and yet I cannot recall a time when I did not *feel* fat.

Perception is not objective. What actually *is* real takes a back seat to what we *experience* as being real. I've never been a fat girl. But I have lived life as one for thirty-something years now.

It strikes me as odd that I, at three, believed being fat was a very negative thing. Three-year-olds have simple jobs. They must learn the difference between red, yellow, and blue, and what sound a kitty makes—and a puppy, and a frog. They must learn their shapes and basic opposites, such as hot and cold, light and dark, little and big. At age three, I was particularly concerned with the difference between fat and thin.

My sister, Erica, six years older than I, was slightly overweight, but incredibly beautiful nonetheless, with wavy chestnut hair and distinctive almond-shaped green eyes. Erica and I share a father only, her mother having been our dad's first wife. As my half-sister, Erica only lived with me on weekends and during the summer. I adored her and eagerly counted down the days until her visits. I can remember craning my neck to see out the car window every week as we drove the twenty-five miles to pick her up from her mother's house, asking every five minutes, "Are we almost there?"

I loved everything about Erica. I loved her with an unconditional, irrational, tag-along little sister type of love, the kind that sees no evil. The kind that sees no fat, in fact, and is confused when it overhears discussions about said fat in hushed, conspiratorial tones. I quickly understood that being fat, or chubby or stocky or thick or pudgy, was undesirable, and perhaps even sinful. Bless me Father, for I have sinned: I've outgrown my jeans and made You worry.

So yes, I believed at age three that being fat was bad. And when I saw how that stupid pink jacket made my belly look, I decided then and there it would have to go. When we got home from preschool, I ran up to my room and nearly ripped the jacket in my haste to get it off. I threw it under my bed and hid myself under my Holly Hobby bedspread, pinching the skin of my belly until I left stinging red welts in the shape of toddler fingers.

From that day on, I was at war with myself. I had been listening closely, as children are apt to do, and I knew food had something to do with fatness. Too much food equaled extra fat on one's body, and I would have no extra fat. Not for all the butter cookies in the world.

In preschool, snack time was an event. Thirty sticky-fingered children sat in miniature chairs at round, miniature tables, awaiting our ration of butter cookies and orange juice. The boys like piranhas, ate them whole, making loud crunching noises and opening their mouths to reveal partially chewed cookies, thereby grossing out the girls, who ate theirs delicately with one raised pinky. If you were a girl, you placed the donut-shaped cookie on your finger like a cookie ring, and nibbled the edges ever so gingerly, in competition to see which girl could make her cookie last the longest.

I was painfully aware, at three, that I was not particularly girly. I wanted to be like my twin friends, Kerri and Kristine. Their hair was always straight and sleek and shiny, and their pigtails hung down perfectly on either side of their heads. My hair was cut in layers, and my pigtails never matched. One side was always higher, slightly forward, and sticking out of the elastic like a tuft of chicken feather. Kerri and Kristine wore perfect matching ensembles, with ribbons and headbands to match. Kerri and Kristine were gentle and feminine and quiet, and giggled shyly when the boys said bad words. Kerri and Kristine were small and dainty in my perception, and I was anything but, with my muscular legs and blonde hairy arms and chicken feather pigtails.

I look at class photos from those early years, and I look no different from my friends. But at age three, and at every age that followed, there was no convincing me of that fact. I was different. I was awkward. And there was entirely too much of me.

I didn't know much about God as a young child. My mother had been raised in the Catholic Church, and it was all she knew, and neither of us particularly cared for church when we went on the obligatory holidays like Christmas and Easter. Church was long and dull and uninspiring, sort of like a routine trip to the dentist. Sometimes we went regularly for weeks on end, when Mom got a bug up her skirt and decided we needed some religion. Then she would grow as bored as I was, and we would stop going as abruptly as we had started.

When we did go, I would sit beside Mom in the hard wooden pew, trying to pay attention for the first twenty minutes, like a good little girl. Finally, the boredom would get to me and I would begin to bite my fingernails for lack of any better pastime. Then Mom would pull out an empty bank deposit envelope from her purse, discreetly unfold it to create a blank canvas, and hand me a pen. "You can draw," she would whisper, "but only if you draw something about God." So I would sit quietly for several minutes, because I didn't know anything about God. Neither did Mom, yet we both felt we *should* know something about God. After all, we were Catholic, by virtue of the fact that we lived in Joliet, Illinois, a very Catholic town. I would draw a cross, sometimes with the little man on it, sometimes without. Then I would shove the bank envelope back into mom's purse and bite my nails for the remaining forty-five minutes.

After church, we would go to Dunkin' Donuts for soup, which seems odd now, but at the time, they had some pretty decent chicken noodle soup that my mother and I would crave. We sat at the counter, facing racks of multicolored donuts on display. I watched what Mom ate. Mom was skinny, so if she ate soup, I figured it was okay for me to eat soup. There was one horrible Sunday, though, when my grandma, known to us all as Mimi, came along. I finished my soup and asked for a pink-frosted donut with sprinkles. I have no idea what could have possessed me, perhaps the fact that I was a five-year-old on a growth spurt. I had no sooner asked my mother for the donut than Mimi put her crooked, arthritic hand over mine on the pink laminate counter and said, "Oh, noooo, honey. You'll get fat!" Mom assured me it was fine for me to have a donut if I was still hungry, but Mimi's words echoed in my brain and made my face sting with sudden, blazing heat. There would be no donut for me. Not for many years, in fact.

In truth, I was a little girl of average build and stature. I was not thin or wiry—nor was I prone to chunkiness. I was medium. Regular-sized. My jeans were neither "husky" nor "slim"—and this caused me great distress once I knew there was such a distinction. "Slim" seemed like something little girls *should* be. I was certain Kerri and Kristine wore "slim" jeans.

I learned early, as all kids must, that life isn't fair. The fact that I could not have a younger sibling seemed a great injustice. I was too young to understand why Daddy's vasectomy should be such a roadblock to achieving this goal. I was also in too much denial to admit that Mommy and Daddy were having terrible fights all the time, with Mommy yelling and crying and Daddy throwing things, and that maybe we all wouldn't be living together much longer.

The inevitable divorce happened during my sixth year. Events of that time swirl like black-and-white images in my memory, like an old silent film. There are a few vivid moments, like the day I got off the school bus and found Daddy home instead of Mommy because Mommy had been admitted into a special hospital for sad people; the day I had to choose whose house I wanted to sleep in (the old house with Daddy or the new rental house with Mommy); and the day Daddy came over to the new house where Mommy and I were living and got very angry and hit Mommy, and then became angry at himself and punched himself in the face until he bled out of his nose. Those I remember, in technicolor—with lots and lots of red.

I'm sure it was difficult, maybe even traumatic, but the soul of a child is profoundly resilient, and life just seemed to go on. I still had friends, I still got straight A's, I still made popsicle-stick crafts and went sledding and danced in my bedroom. I saw Daddy on weekends and listened to him say mean things about Mommy, and then I went home and listened to Mommy say mean things about Daddy.

Somehow I learned to tune it out. I don't remember feeling all that sad about our broken home. In fact, I remember feeling guilty about *not* feeling sad. I don't remember being angry at Mom and Dad. I remember being angry at myself. Not for causing their divorce, as several therapists have suggested. Not for not being sad enough. No. I was angry at myself for being fat.

Being fat seemed an efficient catch-all. I needed to be mad at myself, because I couldn't be mad at anyone else. Early on, I came to equate being angry with being mean and believed only mean people got angry. And since I needed a reason to be mad at myself, my self-imposed handicap of imaginary fatness seemed very convenient.

I'd like to say being angry about being fat served its purpose in time, and I got over it. I did not. It got worse. When you begin to tell yourself a lie, day in and day out, two inevitable things occur. One: you become very good at lying. Two: you begin to believe your own lies to the extent that they become your own inarguable truth. Oops.

And so, off we go on a roller-coaster ride of self-loathing, through grade school and middle school and puberty, and round and round we go, and where we'll stop, God only knows.

arrived at puberty the way I arrive at most conclusions: without really meaning to. Each year at Grand Prairie Elementary School, the fifth-grade students were taken on a much-dreaded field trip to the Robert Crown Center in Chicago. On this outing, the girls and the boys were separated so they could learn about the magic of puberty and sexual development. It might as well have been called "What to Expect When Your Body Matures More Quickly than Your Emotions." The girls were sent off to watch filmstrips about getting their periods, growing breasts, and not becoming a mother before high school graduation. The boys were sent off to learn the deep mysteries of manhood, and I suspect, sadly, that nowadays they leave with condoms in the pockets of their jeans. I am sure it was educational. I am kind of sad that I missed out on it, really.

In the middle of fifth grade, I gracefully dismounted from the pommel horse in gym class, landed with my right foot pointing behind me, and heard a loud snap. I spent the next several months in a full-leg cast, scooting everywhere on my backside because I was, for some inexplicable reason, humiliated at the thought of using crutches and felt that crab-walking around the house was far more dignified. I was unable to attend school and instead studied at home with a private tutor. And because Sex Ed is not a subject typically taught one-on-one, I missed out on the lessons my classmates enjoyed on that field trip, while I convalesced at home.

It is interesting to recall how self-conscious I was about my body in those months while I was laid up. My mom warned me that I could "get chubby" if we weren't careful, due to my decreased level of physical activity. Those words somehow came out like blasts of fire from her mouth, and their heat stayed with me, flushing my face each time I replayed them in memory. As the weeks ticked by, I was not concerned about my leg not setting properly or loss of muscle tone or whether I would heal properly and walk upright again. I was concerned only not to get chubby.

I decided that a person who does not walk on two feet does not require solid food, and I reasoned that mainlining orange juice exclusively should be sufficient for my nutrition. I remember counting the days I managed to ingest only orange juice, to the exclusion of all food. I made it to three. I suppose Mom figured it was good I was listening to my body, which was apparently craving calcium-fortified juice; I can't blame her for not noticing my fast. Until that point, I had not given her much reason to worry about my food intake. But at the end of day three, my little game was ruined.

Mom had remarried when I was in third grade to a man named Bill whom she did not love, as an act of financial and emotional desperation. That night, Bill brought home buckets of fried chicken and biscuits. I tried to fight against temptation, but the salty, savory smell filled the room as he entered, armed with paper plates and plastic sporks. I ate a chicken leg and half a biscuit, sitting on the carpet in the family room, watching *Star Search* on television. A little girl sang and danced on the show, kicking spindly toothpick legs all about. I looked at my own legs, one curled under me, one stretched out in white graffitied plaster, a smudge of chicken grease on the knee. *Chubby . . . chubby . . . chubby . . .*

And then it occurred to me: if I can put food in, I can take food out. I remembered Mom telling me how she used to shove her fingers down her throat as a teenager to rid herself of that horrible feeling of fullness. I do not believe my mother was bulimic in the clinical sense; she had been an extremely thin girl and was self-conscious about her bony body. She did, however, inherit her father's "nervous stomach" and sought relief in self-induced vomiting, as her father had for years. I scooted across the family room into the bathroom, pulled myself to a wobbly stand at the sink, bent over, and reached down my throat with the first two fingers of my right hand. I gagged. My eyes watered, and my face flushed. Nothing. I tried again, this time shoving them further down and promising myself I would not retract them until I threw up, no matter how strong the urge to pull my fingers out. Nothing. I cried, feeling like a fat failure who couldn't even throw up right. I decided I would never eat again. Never.

Of course, my will power at age eleven had not yet developed into the potentially dangerous bullheadedness it would later become, and I resumed eating as usual within a week. I remained paranoid of becoming chubby. I designed elaborate calisthenics routines, which I would perform each night on my makeshift bed on the family room floor after my mother and stepfather had gone upstairs to bed. It must have worked, because despite my inactivity during the months I wore the cast, I did not gain a pound. But the relief would not last long.

We all seem to move from trauma to trauma, or maybe just from drama to drama, when we are in adolescence. Everything that happens is extreme; we're extremely sad or extremely excited or extremely confused. Blame it on raging hormones. Take the raging hormones and combine them with a rather extreme personality—terribly sensitive, given to fits of inexplicable tears, obsessive, precocious, perfectionist—and you have a recipe for disaster. Something brewed just under the surface in me at age eleven—something menacing. Something like an eating disorder, but dormant—a sleeping monster waiting to be awakened to his opportunity to pounce.

It's too bad I missed that field trip to the Crown Center, or I might have been better prepared for the no good, awful, horrible, terrible Tuesday in spring 1987 when I stopped playing on my jungle gym for a quick trip to the bathroom, pulled up my bib overall shorts after using the toilet, tossed my braid over my shoulder, and noticed a few drops of red in the toilet. I knew what it was; Mom had always been open about this sort of thing. By age six, I knew that each month a mommy's body gets rid of the "baby house" it would have needed if God had chosen to begin growing a baby in her belly. What I didn't understand is why God would ever dream that an eleven-year-old would need such a house. I wasn't a mommy. I was a child.

I felt betrayed by my body. How dare it grow up faster than I wanted it to? I wasn't ready for this hassle. And I was somehow fully and painfully aware that I was the first of my friends to get my period.

I took this opportunity, standing over the toilet in horror and disbelief, to pray. "Oh dear God, please make this go away!" I hoped against hope I had somehow injured myself and was bleeding internally, but I knew better. My tummy felt funny— soft, spongy, and sore. So I amended my prayer to "Oh dear God, please don't let this make me fat." Odd. I don't know what caused me to fear that the one thing might automatically trigger the other. I only know the fear of imminent weight gain gripped me that afternoon, something fierce.

I was moving swiftly into womanhood, and I wanted no part of it. I wanted to be a child—androgynous, untethered, carefree. I wanted to climb trees and ride my bike and play Barbies. It seemed absurd that a person who still wanted to play Barbies would be a person who could have a baby. The way I saw it, maxi pads and a hot pink teddy bear lunch box did not belong in the same backpack.

I was caught between worlds: I was not yet an adult and apparently no longer a child. The problem was, I hadn't yet gotten around to *being* a child, and now I felt I had missed my opportunity altogether.

By age eleven, I had grown into a convenient role in my familial system, which therapists would later refer to as the Symptom Bearer. Everyone in my family was chaotic. My world was swirling around me, tornado-like, and I was caught in its cold, roaring eye. I needed guidance, and my parents did the best they could. I was a mess, didn't know why, and had too few words to express what was going on inside my head. All I knew, by eleven, was that I hated my body with a vile hatred so intense it frightens me now to recall it. And so, at the start of sixth grade, the inevitable happened: my emotional dam broke, and I became a basket case.

Sixth grade was the start of junior high school, which meant changing classrooms, multiple teachers, pre-algebra, study hall in lieu of recess, home ec and wood shop and drug awareness and health class. It also meant students were suddenly required to change clothes and shower for gym, now that we were old enough to sweat and to stink.

I cannot begin to express the terror this induced. I was a freak, remember—a freak with sore nubs of new breasts, an oily t-zone, and hips, the first promise of an hourglass figure I would always despise. And as if all of these deformities weren't enough, I hemorrhaged once a month. I could think of nothing more freakish than that.

I agonized over the gym class scenario for the entire summer before sixth grade. I plotted, I schemed, I racked my brain to come up with an out. I even tried to re-break my ankle by jumping off of the top bar of my jungle gym, the top of the stairs at home, the tallest slide at the playground. Nothing.

My class schedule had the major academics in the morning during the first four periods—reading, language arts, math, science—with gym to follow during fifth period, three days a week. So, three days a week, I became suddenly ill—headaches, dizziness, nausea, toothache, hangnail, whatever it took to escape fifth period. I would end up in the nurse's office, or in the main office with an ice pack, or just hiding out in a bathroom stall, my feet pulled up onto the toilet seat. Or, when I could pull it off, I played hooky and stayed home altogether. My report card from sixth grade shows I was absent a total of forty-three days.

Eventually, I was found out. Someone came looking for me, and I was escorted to gym class. Luckily, everyone had already changed clothes and was warming up, running laps around the gym. I changed quickly in the locker room, by myself, and fell into a brisk jog beside my friends. Being with my friends usually calmed me. I liked to make people laugh and was pretty good at it. My fear was that I would be laughed *at*—which is why, when the gym teacher blew the whistle for us to head to the showers, I freaked. I couldn't breathe. My muscles felt they had turned to concrete. I clenched my fists into white-knuckled balls of anxiety. And I bolted.

I ran out of the gym to the bathroom down the hall and

locked myself in a stall. Mrs. Klint, my sweet gym teacher, followed and stood at the other side of the stall door, talking me down. "Are you sick?" she asked.

"I think so," I replied, lamely.

"Let's get your clothes changed, and then I'll give you a pass to go visit the nurse."

I knew I needed more time, to be sure that everyone else had showered and changed. "I need a few minutes, please!"

This scenario played out once more before I was finally sent to speak with Mrs. Packer, the school social worker. I didn't know what a social worker was, or why I needed one, but I knew her office felt like the safest room in the school. It was smallish, like an oversized closet, and the cinder block walls had been painted lavender and adorned with posters promoting self-esteem and assertiveness. There were boxes of tissue everywhere, and I quickly learned that this was a crying room.

Mrs. Packer seemed like a safe person in whom to confide —her eyes were kind and she leaned in when I spoke, and she cooed with compassion in all the right places. I eventually spilled everything. I told her I was a fat, clumsy, bleeding, gushing freak of nature. I told her that my mom and my stepdad fought constantly and that he hated me. And I told her, in no uncertain terms, that I could not, would not, change my clothes or shower in front of my friends. She took her cue from that assertion and probed a bit on the body topic. I told her I hated mine and would like to cut it up. Evidently, that's not something to say casually to a social worker.

Mrs. Packer probably knew then what I know now: that there is a greater risk for eating disorders and emotional problems for girls who undergo early puberty, when the pressures experienced by all adolescents are intensified by experiencing, seemingly alone, these early physical changes, including normal increased body fat.

Within two days I had an appointment with a child psychiatrist. I was prescribed Xanax for anxiety and declared "emotionally unstable." I wasn't sure exactly what that meant, although the connotation was clear: I was bonkers. I didn't care. It meant I had a doctor's note that allowed me to be picked up from school every day after my first four classes and taken home. My only other academic class, social studies, was taken as a home study course.

And so, in the twelfth year of my life, I got to be a crazy person. I got to be sick, sad, confused, troubled, a head case, a mess of symptoms. It's a role nearly everyone tries on at least once in her life, to see if it fits. I found out, by the end of the school year, that I didn't care to play the part. I grew tired of being checked out and looked into and charted about.

A fantastically convenient thing happened over the following summer: my friends grew breasts and got their periods. At the time, I decided that was really all I needed to happen—that, and for my mom to divorce my stepdad, which she did, that same summer. I told my mother I didn't need the Xanax anymore. I refused to go talk to Doctor Whoever-He-Was ever again. Mom agreed on one condition: I had to attend seventh grade all day long, no tutors, no unexcused absences, no calls home from the social worker warning my mother of my borderline suicidal ideation.

I thought that was fair enough.

Choose Whom You Will Serve

I arrived in high school unscathed, save for the usual bumps and bruises—puppy love gone south, backbiting girlfriends, that sort of thing. I still hated my body, but I had grown to believe hating my body was simply part of *having* a body. I toyed with dieting, fasted for a day or two once in a while, and then gave in to the voracious appetite of a teenager who was still growing and spent up to twelve hours a day at school, rehearsing for plays and musicals and choirs and bands. The somewhat erratic eating, often late at night, caused me to reach my lifetime highest weight of 138 pounds at age sixteen.

It was an odd time to be me. I was discovering my talents for music and theater, which was encouraging and quite good for parts of my fragile ego. I was also coming to learn about the flip side of the performer's ego—the side that collapses into a pile of tired, defeated dust when the lights go off after the play, after the last note is played or sung in the concert.

Friends and family were supportive, always bringing me flowers at performances and telling me how much they enjoyed whatever I had done. A healthy person might enjoy this positive attention, might feel a little inflated by the accolades. A healthy person might not have a horrible undercurrent of self-deprecation, competing with the praise. I, unfortunately, was not a healthy person, even then.

Friends might tell me how well I sang the national anthem at the basketball game or how much they enjoyed my performance in the spring musical, and immediately the voice in my brain would chime in: *You'd better hope they never find out what a fraud you are. They think you have real talent. You've got them fooled. You're nothing—nothing.* Always in these shaming, self-defeating moments, I was suddenly and inexplicably fat—fatter than I had been the moment before. I would grab the flesh of my belly, or inner thigh, and pinch until the tears stung my eyes, leaving bluish-yellow bruises the following day.

But these were only moments. They were not yet a way of life, as they would become. In high school, the good outweighed the bad, and the light outshone the darkness, for the most part. I loved high school. The many creative outlets—band, choir, theater, literary magazine, speech team—kept me on just enough of a high to keep me from slipping over to the dark side. And, notably, God Himself was wooing me.

In the summer before my sophomore year, my friend Vanessa invited me to attend a weeklong Bible camp in Saugatauk, Michigan, where she worked as a counselor. She told me it would be lots of fun, that we would swim and canoe and master ropes courses and flirt with cute boys from other states. And she assured me that, although it was a Bible camp, you didn't have to get born again or anything crazy like that. In other words, come for the fun, stay for the boys, and as for the Jesus piece, well, you could take Him or leave Him.

As it turned out, I took Him, and He took me. I had no idea what to expect, my only experience with God being the boring

Catholic masses I'd attended as a young girl. This was different. The music was cool, contemporary. Nobody preached in Latin. Nobody tried to tell me how guilty I was or that I couldn't read the Bible on my own. They taught me, that week, that I could pray to God directly—with no priest or Virgin Mary required as a go-between. I liked that. They made it sound as if prayer was simply an ongoing conversation between my heavenly Father and me. I wanted that. Who wouldn't want to be a friend of God?

I may have oversimplified these messages, but simple was what I needed just then. I needed to know that God loved me, that because of Jesus and the cross, we're cool, God and me. I needed to know that nothing I had ever done was too much for Him to forgive. I needed to know what God says about me— that I am His creation, His child, His friend, His beloved—and needed to hear that the very fact that He created me and gave me life means I have value.

I came back from camp and began my sophomore year of high school. School was the same, my classmates were the same, my day-to-day life was the same. But my heart was changed. It was new. I had hope about my future I could not explain. I was suddenly bothered, in a righteous way, by my friends' racial jokes. I found my capacity to love others in spite of their prickliness had grown tenfold. I was quick to forgive when I was wronged. And I was acutely aware of the fact that I was not alone.

I truly believe God babies us a little when we are new believers. He shows up in some obvious ways to keep us chugging along when we might start to sputter. I'll never forget the day I was climbing the stairs at school, en route to English class, and it hit me suddenly that I had forgotten we were having a quiz that morning on *Hamlet*. I had been at rehearsal all evening the night before, and I hadn't done the reading. Since I was a perfectionist prone to anxiety, this would have been freakout time in the past. Instead, as I climbed the stairs, I prayed, "God, I know You are with me. I'm so sorry I screwed up and blew off my reading. I need a second chance. Can You please make sure we have a substitute teacher for some reason today?" It was a random thing to ask God to do, not to mention cocky, to ask Him to cover my backside when I had neglected my studying. But I had such a sense of confidence in Him, it didn't occur to me that He might not answer the prayer. I just figured He would. I wasn't surprised when I rounded the corner into the classroom and saw the substitute teacher writing his name on the dry-erase board.

There is a spiritual high you experience when you first surrender your heart and life to Christ. It is much like being in love; life is rosy, even sadness has an undercurrent of untouchable bliss, and there is always a song in your heart. Everything is significant; everything is a sign from God. Every word spoken to you, if you like it, is prophetic, so you think. God is on the throne of your life, and you are just riding a wave.

Then life happens. It always does. You fail a test or your boyfriend cheats or your butt looks big in your prom dress. And suddenly God seems to have moved, leaving no forwarding address. The counselors warned us about these "valley experiences" at camp. They told us we would go home, high on Jesus, we would enjoy the splendor for a while, and then we would hit a plateau—or a wall—and wonder where God had gone.

On the van ride home from camp, one of the counselors had us each write a postcard, addressed to ourselves at home. We were to encourage ourselves with the Word of God, and then the counselor would hang on to the cards and drop them in the mail at some future point. This was my first lesson in the uncannily perfect timing of God. I came home one day, feeling discouraged and downtrodden. Some of my friends had been making fun of my faith, telling me I had sold out to a dated, irrelevant message of redemption that simply wasn't true. I was growing frustrated and labored under the false belief that I was singlehandedly responsible for evangelizing my circle of friends at Plainfield High School. I was feeling like a failure, praying like crazy, and sensing only silence from God.

On my way up to the house, I checked the mailbox and prayed that God would speak to me through the mail. I still do this; on particularly dark days, I believe Jesus might send me something in the mail or e-mail that will be my answer. He also uses billboards, TV commercials, and the radio in my car. I love that about Him. That afternoon, I reached in and found only one piece of mail: the encouragement card I had written to myself on the way home from camp, five months before. I wept for joy. God was good. God could hear me and see what was going on with me. And suddenly I felt lighter, less fat than I had felt before reaching in for the mail. Go figure.

I'd like to say God kept sending me postcards and I never felt fat again. But that would be ridiculous. The truth is, life did take over, and the evil self-deprecating thoughts continued and grew stronger. The thing is, once we have the tools—the Word of God, prayer, the power that comes from knowing Truth—we are responsible to employ them. We are told in Ephesians 6 to "put on the whole armor of God." This is action. This is something we must intentionally and consciously *do*, daily. I didn't. I was a busy, overextended teenager, caught up in crushes and proms and concerts and plays. And changing the way I had thought for fifteen years was not going to happen overnight. It would take time and tenacity. And I, busy and distracted, chose not to invest much of either.

My grandmother, Mimi, used to say that we "wear a groove in our brains" from thinking the same thoughts over and over again. She claimed this was why she made such a habit of worrying; those synapses in her brain fired out of habit, just following that same old "groove." Mimi may not have had higher education in psychology, but she was on to something. Only later, slumped in a series of therapists' cushy couches and leather chairs, would I understand the principle of Cognitive-Behavioral Therapy, which is a fancy term for learning to "think outside the groove" and thereby change one's behavior.

By the time I was in high school, I had been thinking in the same unhealthy groove for years. I experienced myself as fat, freakish, clumsy, awkward, loud, stupid, lazy, undisciplined, fake, superficial, and socially inept—despite evidence to the contrary. My negative thoughts were beyond logic. Those grooves had worn deep.

I needed to choose a new way of thinking, but I made a sort of non-decision—an unconscious, uninformed choice *not* to choose at all. I did not choose Truth. But I also can't remember choosing the Lie. Maybe it was more of a sin of passivity at that point. The lie had chosen *me*, and I chose not to fight against its talons and wriggle myself free. And sadly, right then would have been the time to do it.

———

I was overtly conscious of my butt throughout high school. I was equally conscious of everyone else's, comparing them with mine. Other girls would pass me in the hall, and I would turn abruptly enough to induce whiplash, as if I were a dog and a shiny red car had driven past, and check the back end. I am not proud of this.

I am even less proud to admit I still do this, to this day. I do it in the mall, on the street. I check my rear in the mirror more often and more thoroughly than I check my face. I'm not sure, really, what I check it for. To see if it has grown? Or morphed?

Or changed shape? To see if my greatest fear has come true and I am suddenly trailing a gigantic great divide everywhere I go? I'm not sure which is the sadder commentary here—that I check my rear end incessantly, or that its overdevelopment is my greatest fear.

Now that I am a parent, the uncontrollable expansion of my backside is no longer my greatest fear. It was in high school. And so, just after graduation, I decided to take matters into my own hands and make sure my greatest fear was far behind me. Farther behind me than my behind itself.

I hadn't been sure whether or not I wanted to go away for college. I had always been a bit of a homebody, always the kid who couldn't make it all night at a sleepover, who would call at three in the morning for a ride home. I grew out of that anxiety by the time I was in junior high school, but the idea of leaving home for months seemed daunting, even at age seventeen. I think I was more afraid of leaving my mother than of leaving home. Mom had been divorced from my stepfather for five years by then, and I wasn't sure she would fare well if left to her own devices.

It is worth noting that my mother was an adult. It is also worth noting that I, over the years, had somehow taken it upon my teenage shoulders to reverse our roles. When she was going out, I wanted to know when she would be home. If she was out late, I expected a phone call. When she didn't call, I was ticked. I often felt the urge to ground her to her room for the weekend, forgetting she was a forty-five-year-old woman, and my mother to boot.

As tethered as I felt to home, I also felt drawn to the idea of spreading my wings—ever so slightly—and going away to school. All of my friends were going away, and I was not above the influence of peer pressure. I wasn't sure what I wanted to study, and so, in keeping with my personal tradition of deferring to others' opinions, I asked my teachers and friends what I should be when I grew up.

My choir director, whom I admired and adored, affirmed that I would make a great music teacher. She asked me to consider a small private school just twenty-five miles away—North Central College in Naperville, Illinois. I considered it and discovered that it was extremely expensive. "But you can get performance scholarships, Jena," Miss Moore said. "You've just got to audition. You'll never know unless you try."

The old voice in my head chimed in, as if on cue: *Still fooling people, aren't you? She thinks you have talent. She thinks you could get a scholarship. If you go audition and they laugh at you, she'll know what a fraud you've been.*

I pushed beyond the voice. I really wanted to go to North Central. Naperville is a posh little town with a bustling downtown area full of chic boutiques and coffee houses, and if I stayed on campus I would be far enough away from home to prove to myself that I could be semi-on-my-own, but still close enough to come home on weekends to check on my (fully capable, fully grown) mother. I *really* wanted to go to North Central.

In my weekly private voice lessons, I prepared two audition pieces—one in Italian, one in English. I practiced like crazy, nearly *made* myself crazy, and auditioned. I not only got in, I received three separate scholarships. And for a few months leading up to my freshman year in college, the defeating voice in my head fell *almost* silent.

My mom was relieved I had chosen a school so close to home. She was dating a man at the time, and that helped to soften the blow of my departure from the nest. Still, it had been just the two of us—"you and me against the world," as Mom would often phrase it—for five years, and I was nervous about leaving her alone.

I have always taken on responsibility that was not mine and was far too much for me. As a little girl of seven, I used to place my hand on my mother's shoulder and tell her I was sure she'd be able to pay the mortgage somehow. "We'll make it, Mommy," I would say, all the while worrying about what our lives would look like if we didn't. Mom has her share of responsibility to take for our premature reversal of dependency, but I believe much of it has to do with my personality. There is some pride involved, for me so haughtily to imagine I actually have the capacity to hold the world around me together, against all odds. It's strange to have low self-esteem and a Messiah complex all at once, but I manage.

I got a job at the Gap a block away from campus and used my employee discount to stock up on clothes I thought a college girl should wear—vintage-washed jeans and preppy oxford shirts and a green nylon backpack.

An old photo, one of my mom's favorites, shows me standing in her kitchen, wearing denim overall shorts, a striped button-down shirt, a green corduroy baseball cap and ponytail, with my backpack slung over one shoulder. My face is tan, my blond hair bleached lighter by the summer sun, and I look the very picture of youthful glow. At the time, I saw only a chubby girl destined to grow chubbier still with the dreaded "freshman fifteen," and I decided then and there that college was going to mean more than just independence and a higher education. It was going to mean a lower number on the scale—*no matter what.*

I arrived on campus on a Thursday and met my roommate, Ally. She was all of four-foot-eleven, and she had a head of short spiral curls like Shirley Temple and a smallish, squeaky voice. She had come south to Naperville from Harvard, Illinois, a dairy farming community known for a giant bronze cow statue in the middle of town. I thought we'd get along; she seemed nice. She probably thought I was a little strange, but she laughed at my jokes and mostly kept quiet, which suited me fine. After all, I had a busy trimester ahead that included eleven courses, lessons and performing ensembles, plus my part-time job at the Gap, and the most important task of all: losing weight.

Luckily, I quickly found a distraction: a cute guy. I had only been on campus for one day when I met him. Mike Watson was a senior music education major, finishing up his final trimester of classes before he began his student teaching gigs. He strolled into the choir room in Pfeiffer Hall and parked his lanky boy-man body at the piano to lead vocal warm-ups. He was precisely my type: artsy, talented, quirky, with that geeky sort of attractiveness I find easier on the eyes than blatant hunky sex appeal. I was smitten within minutes.

He had voluptuous lips for a guy—like twin pillows that worked themselves together in an odd, twisted grin, parting when he began to sing, revealing an orthodontically perfected smile and a smooth, well-trained baritone. He was clean-cut and tidy, far more so than was the trend in the mid-1990s grunge era, and I instantly loved that about him. It was obvious he was well liked by everyone in the music department, but I hoped desperately that I was the only one to find him positively irresistible. Soon those around us began to observe the chemistry between us.

"So," Ally would say as I returned to our room after classes, "did you get to hang out with lover boy after rehearsals?" And

I would giggle as she batted her eyelashes, mocking me. The whole gee-why-do-you-ask routine didn't hold up for long, and most of these girl-talk sessions ended up with me flinging myself across one of our extra-narrow beds, long hair spilling toward the floor, breathlessly sighing, "Isn't he wonderful? I mean it, Al, isn't he just seriously, like, *the* perfect guy? For me, I mean?" And she would humor me for a while, smirking, before finally pushing me off the bed and telling me to go take a cold shower before I overheated. My infatuation amused her. I was as giddy as Gidget in love.

Within the first week on campus, students were required to complete paperwork for their meal packages. This had been prepaid as part of my tuition, but I was expected to fill out forms to obtain my meal card, which would be used to purchase dinners and snacks in the dining hall and in the campus social hub, "The Cage." Without this card, I would not be able to get food. I figured such a dilemma would be helpful in my crusade against my first twenty pounds and did not, therefore, complete the paperwork. I had no meal card, which was a great excuse for not having meals. Instead, I used my earnings from my job to buy jars of baby food and bags of rice cakes and cases of Diet Coke. I stocked my little fridge in the dorm with these diet essentials, much to Ally's chagrin.

"Seriously, Jena," she would scoff, with one raised brow, "baby food? Are we eighteen *years* old, or eighteen months?"

"Whatever," I would laugh. "Don't knock it 'til you try it." I figured, being a solid size eight, I could easily laugh off any judgment by playing up the quirkiness of my personality. Since I wasn't particularly skinny, surely no one would think much of a teenager living off of baby food. Besides, mom and I had eaten vanilla custard baby food for years, as a treat. It wasn't *that* weird.

It didn't take long for my jeans to grow loose on me. And that, of course, is when things got particularly twisted. Once an anoretic begins to see results of her little disappearing act, the trap snaps. Euphoria sets in. Chemical changes occur in the brain, and she begins to experience a high, much like the buzzing hum of mania. The sensation of hunger is anesthetized by the release of endorphins like one experiences after a run or after a tennis match or after sex. Less scientifically, if you are a girl raised in the thin-is-in culture, it is easy to become addicted to the feeling of growing smaller and smaller by the day. You love the sensation of swimming in your jeans, the way the waistband twists on your hips with each step, the way you have to keep pulling them up when they fall.

An eating disorder, in the beginning, is like being in love. Everything else takes a backseat to your new passion. If your quirky "habit" begins to worry or annoy or even repel people, so be it. So be it, you think, because at least you have *this*. Who needs them, when you have *this*?

This sort of thinking is unconscious at first. I wouldn't have consciously chosen a disorder over my family and friends and every other goal in my life. I wouldn't have consciously chosen an eating disorder, period. And yet, I did. And once you make that initial choice, it is ever so easy to choose it time and time again.

The dining hall happened to be attached to Rall Hall, the freshman girls' dorm where we lived. I did not appreciate this convenience. All hours of the day, our dorm room smelled like chocolate chip cookies and beef tacos. Mornings, we awakened to the aroma of Belgian waffles prepared by ravenous students at the do-it-yourself waffle makers. Ally and some of the girls from our floor began conspiring to get me down to the dining hall. "Come on, Jena," they would coo in sing-song tones, "it's sundae night!" I would say I needed to study. "Jena, the salad bar looked really good today; if you use the fat-free dressing, you could have, like, a really healthy dinner." I would say thanks, but I had rehearsal or work. Ultimately, one of the girls would try another tactic: "You know, Jena, you're starting to look kind of, well, *gross*. You really should come eat dinner with us. Just for tonight." And I, guilty and caught, would tag along and pretend to become nauseous. "I'm really sorry, guys," I'd say, "I've just had this weird stomach thing lately. Maybe next time."

I did not enjoy the lying and sneaking around. I felt like a criminal—or worse, an addict. But this sense of conviction did not last long. I spent most of my time concentrating on the changes taking place in my body, noting every new bone and symptom with glee. This seems weird now. All I can say, thinking back, is that my need to be *thin* seamlessly morphed into a need to be *sick*. This was right around the time that obsession became disorder—when my period stopped, when I began growing fur on my belly and arms (the body grows this soft, downy lanugo to keep itself warm in the absence of insulating body fat), when the blackouts became more frequent and severe.

I had begun to avoid going home, so as not to be lectured or to worry my mom. On one visit in October, she had mentioned that I looked too skinny and asked me, in jest, if I was "becoming anorexic again" (the diagnosis had been tossed around when I first showed symptoms at age eleven). I had laughed it off and blamed the weight loss on a stressful schedule, and then I beat a hasty return to my little cocoon at school, where I settled in for the duration, away from the watchful eye, determined to meet my goal. Trouble was, it was a fairly open-ended goal from the outset.

Originally, I had wanted to lose weight. After the first twenty pounds had fallen off in a month, I could have certainly said I'd met that primary initiative. But a sinister, twisted paradigm shift had occurred: I no longer wanted simply to get thinner; I wanted to *shrink*, in every sense of the word. Actually, it was no longer a matter of what I wanted. It was, after those first twenty pounds, a matter of pure, unmitigated obsession.

Mike and I had been hanging around more and more, mostly with our group of music friends, but I relished every moment. Soon we were talking on the phone until all hours of the night, me giggling and whispering in my dorm room with the corded phone hidden under the covers while Ally tried to sleep in the next bed. When I was with Mike or talking with him, I was almost normal. I was a giddy, carefree college kid instead of a starving, freezing, aching waif growing weaker and old before my time.

It is painful to reflect on my self-sabotaging behavior during this time. The two things I thought I wanted so desperately—Mike and thinness—were mutually exclusive. Mike was drawn to my bubbly personality, my sense of fun, and possibly my butt—and I was systematically losing all three.

When Mike and I did spend time together one on one, I felt myself most alive. I had a giant crush on him and butterflies in my stomach along with all the pills and the hollow emptiness. When I was with Mike, I wasn't as easily distracted by my thighs or my reflection or the amount of space I inhabited, because I focused on his wonderful laugh, his incredibly thick hair, his dimples, and the way I wished he would slip his arm around my waist, pull me close, and kiss me as I had never been kissed before.

We went out to dinner at a Chili's one night after a rehearsal, and as we waited for a table in the crowded restaurant and my stomach lurched and churned at the smell of fajitas from a nearby table, Mike leaned in close behind me, his hands on my hips. I felt his breath against the back of my neck as he said,

"Mmm. You smell good."

My skin erupted in goosebumps, and the butterflies in my stomach did backflips. I leaned back, falling into his warm flannel-clad chest, and said, "So do you."

There we were, his hands on my hips, me leaning into his chest, smelling one another's pheromones and cologne. It might have seemed only natural for him to lean in, tenderly turn my chin toward his face, and kiss me gently and warmly. In my imagination, he did. In reality, a hostess with abominable timing called us to our table.

I ordered fajitas, figuring I could simply munch on a few grilled vegetables from the platter, avoiding the meat and tortillas altogether. Mike said nothing about my eating habits, as we played footsie under the table and laughed at one another's jokes. In the moment, I was more distracted by my lust for him than by the frightening plate of food before me.

He drove me back to my dorm in his red Jeep as we sang along in harmony to a CD of a cappella music. When we pulled up in front of the building, we lingered, as usual. We cracked jokes, we sang, we touched one another's arms when we spoke. I wanted to scream, *Just kiss me already!*

Finally, Mike reached out, swept my long hair off my forehead and tucked it behind my ear, caressed my cheek softly, lifted my chin ever so gently, and kissed me, long and soft and slow. My knees were shaking, and I was grateful I was sitting down. I was also suddenly aware of how utterly unsexy I was. As we kissed, I allowed my mind to wander into forbidden territory, and I imagined him pulling me close, removing my jacket, and finding—nothing. Bones. A pale, hollow chest. It struck me as strange just then, how desperately I found myself wishing I had a few curves.

As it turned out, Mike was a gentleman that evening, and the kiss remained just that. I slammed the door, jogged up the sidewalk into the dorm, climbed the stairs with my still-shaky legs, and entered my room in a whirlwind of giggles and heat. I fell onto my bed dramatically, heart pounding both from the afterglow of the most amazing kiss of my young life and from the stomach-twisting concoction of diet pills floating through my bloodstream.

"Ally, I love my life," I gushed as my sleepy roommate rolled her eyes. "I do. I love it. Everything about it. I love life!"

"Everything?" Ally yawned, challenging me.

"Everything!" I said. "Life is so unbelievably *good*."

"Glad to hear it," Ally said dryly, not bothering to open her eyes. "So eat something, why don't you? Good night."

Mike and I continued to meet for dinner, to talk for hours over the phone, to cast each other flirtatious glances in rehearsals. With him, I felt vibrant, and there were moments I almost forgot I was in self-destruct mode. And then I attended a choral clinic at my old high school with a grad student named Mary, with whom I sang in the North Central Women's Chorale. During the lunch hour, she and I drove to a Mexican restaurant in downtown Plainfield, and she addressed me directly over a basket of homemade tortilla chips.

"I hope you won't think this is too weird, but I've been wanting to talk to you," she said, dipping a chip into the tiny bowl of fresh salsa.

I braced myself for yet another lecture about my dramatic weight loss. "Okay," I said. "Go ahead."

"Well, Mike and I have been pretty good friends for a few years now," she began. "And I know how much you like him."

"Am I that obvious?" I said, blushing.

"Well, yeah," she smiled, "but he totally encourages it, so it's not like he's not putting vibes out there, too."

"Okay," I said. "So we like each other. Is that bad?"

Hollow

"Well, " Mary said, stalling as she finished chewing a mouthful of chips. "I wanted to make sure that you knew, you know, everything. Like, how Mike operates."

"I don't get it," I said.

"Mike is . . . a great guy," Mary said, laughing nervously. "Mike is a really great guy, so don't think I'm not saying that he's not a good person."

"But?"

"But," Mary said, poking the ice cubes in her water glass with her straw, "Mike . . . always has two girls in his life."

"Two girls?"

"Yeah. Mike always has a girlfriend and a girl friend," she said, separating the last two words for emphasis.

"Like a friend who is a girl?" I asked, beginning to feel sick.

"Exactly," Mary said. "Somehow I get the feeling you didn't know that—and you didn't know Mike has been dating Kelly Clinton for two years."

"What?" I shrieked. "Mike has a girlfriend?"

"A pretty serious one," Mary said firmly. "Like, he's close with her family and everything, and they've talked about marriage. So . . . I know this must hurt to hear, and you are *such* a sweet girl. I didn't want you to fall for him too hard."

"Too late!" I blurted, my face hot and red.

"I'm really sorry, sweetie," Mary said, reaching across the table to place her hand over mine. "But you need to hold out for someone who only needs *one* girl in his life. You deserve that."

That night Mike confirmed over the phone what Mary had said. He even apologized for kissing me, which felt like a verbal smack in the face. I resolved to get over him and spent every day for a month glaring at Kelly Clinton across the choir room, wondering if she had any idea how lucky she was to be the girlfriend. I became acutely aware of how extremely thin she was, and something in my subconscious registered that Mike would rather spend his life with someone who could maintain her teeny body without starving and popping pills and being an obsessive freak. And I believed in my heart that he deserved such a person, rather than an emotionally imbalanced head case like myself.

With the pleasant distraction of Mike out of the way, I resolved to refocus my energy on losing more weight.

Little Girl on Campus

The cereal was my first mistake. I should have shown more restraint. Ally had left a gigantic box of Raisin Bran out on my desk in our dorm, perhaps as a hint. On any other day, I might have tossed the box onto her bed and taken a walk down the hall to visit friends until the temptation passed. But it was Tuesday, my long day. Arriving back in the dorm after eleven at night, starved out of my mind, I watched myself reach into the box and retrieve a handful of dry cereal.

I watched myself pick out the sugarcoated raisins— forbidden fruits—and toss them back into the box. I watched myself eat each dry, sawdusty flake, one by one, heart palpitating with anxiety. Then I watched myself reach in for another handful and shove it into my mouth, raisins and all. I felt my tongue thrill to the treat of real sugar, and watched myself reach in a third time, this time seeking out the forbidden raisins and popping them into my hungry, gaping maw. And then I watched myself panic.

Do the math, do the math! Three handfuls of cereal = two cups? Three? One hundred and ninety calories per cup . . . Or is a handful equal to a half cup? Half or whole, half or whole? Hurry! It's digesting! Do something, do something, do something!

Ipecac. There's a bottle in the first aid kit in the closet. Get it out. Swallow it. All of it. Quick, before you chicken out. Take it. Take it!

I watched myself walk to the closet, take the powerful emetic out of the first aid kit (where it was stored for use as an emergency antidote to accidental poisoning), and guzzle the entire bottle. It was indescribably vile—sickeningly sweet and thick, like rancid maple syrup. (To this day, I cannot smell pancakes without my stomach reacting.) The recommended dosage is one tablespoon, followed immediately by eight ounces of water. Having ingested about ten times the dosage, I never made it to the glass of water.

My stomach began to lurch and churn, and my heart felt funny. Instinctively, I placed my hand over my belly, doubling over, and ran down the hall to the bathroom. Standing before the mirror, my face broken out in a cold sweat, I prayed, *God, what have I done? What did I do? Help me! I'm sorry!*

I lifted up my T-shirt and looked at my reflection. With my belly sunken and hollow beneath my rib cage, I could *see* my stomach churning beneath my skin. I gasped in horror and then fell face first into the sink, my body jolting with each ripping heave. Ipecac is poisonous and can even cause cardiac arrest, as it erodes the heart muscle. (Because it has been so widely abused by anoretics and bulimics, ipecac now must be procured directly from a pharmacist.)

I vomited for what seemed like hours, my knees buckling as I weakened at the sink. I could barely see for the spots floating before my eyes, and my head pounded and felt as though it would explode out through the top of my skull the moment I stood up straight.

The next thing I knew, I was in my bed. It was morning, and I was surprised to be alive.

It is painful, it is physically devastating, it is addicting, and it is shameful. It is laxative abuse, and for the sake of preserving what's left of my own dignity, we will not dwell on the subject. Suffice it to say that I added laxatives to my deadly cocktail early on, having promised myself I would never again touch ipecac. As the story always goes, I started with two to four a day and in time worked myself up to twenty to twenty-five. The bowels are lazy organs, and they'll take any help they can get—and then they will demand more and more help, threatening never again to work on their own.

The horrendous pain of stomach cramps and edema became part of my daily life, another inconvenient price I was willing to pay in order to take up less space on the planet. I believe it was more about punishing myself for eating than it was a means to achieve any real weight loss. I had become not only a sufferer of eating disorders but a student of them as well; I knew that any weight loss caused by laxative abuse was almost all water weight and not fat. Having learned this, at first I decided it wasn't worth it. Then someone made me eat a muffin, and I ran once again to the drugstore in search of the little orange pills. At least water weight was something. Besides, dehydration meant electrolyte imbalance, which could have easily triggered cardiac arrest, which was appealing to me.

This is the part I hadn't planned on. I wasn't prepared for my innocent desire to lose twenty pounds—or forty or sixty—to roll over on its back and bare its teeth as a no-holds-barred attack on my health, causing sickness to move into the territory of Holy Grail. I knew my severely low serum potassium level was a real threat to my life, yet I rather *enjoyed* teetering precariously on that tightrope between a beating and non-beating heart. And so, potassium being a threat to my sickness, I developed a fear of bananas.

Pay attention to what was at work here. I was a good Christian girl. I loved Jesus. I was called, according to my Bible, to be a child of the light. But through something as sinister and twisted as an eating disorder, Satan had begun to draw me over to the dark side, and I didn't even notice.

I'd like to say I was the only girl on campus flirting with death through an eating disorder, but the sad truth is that I was one of many. These illnesses run rampant on college campuses, with many girls even acting out on their symptoms in groups—group fasts, weight-loss contests, even "b/p parties" (binge-purge), at which girls order pizza or raid the cafeteria, only to visit the bathrooms, en masse, to expel the food together.

As God would have it, the Resident Adviser assigned to my floor, a petite, smiling, Florida surfer girl named Carly, was fighting her own eating disorder battle and wasted no time in calling me out on my secret obsession.

As part of a project for my Wellness class, I had been assigned the task of designing a cardiovascular workout routine and charting my progress—heart rate, stamina, et cetera—over a nine-week period. The assignment would make up part of our final grade, and everyone in the class was assigned the same project. For me, it was the perfect opportunity to exercise obsessively at odd hours of the night without drawing attention to myself or causing any extraneous concern from my friends.

With a class and rehearsal schedule that kept me running from building to building twelve hours a day, it was easy to explain why I had to work out late at night, when everyone else on my floor was hanging out in the TV lounge or studying. Ally and I shared the room at the far end of the third-floor hall, the very last room before the back stairs. Those back stairs became my late-night gym, where I performed my elaborate step aerobic routine for hours, uninterrupted. It was *my* time alone with my increasingly disorganized thoughts, which marched rhythmically in my head, a cadence of words echoing with the screeching of my gym shoes on the vinyl tiled stairs.

Every twenty minutes or so, a girl might come down to use the bathroom at our end of the hall, and smile and wave to me on her way in and out. One night, just past midnight, one of those girls happened to be Carly. Coming out of the bathroom, she started down the hall to her room but stopped mid-stride and came back to sit on the top stair, wiping her just-washed hands on her sweatpants.

"Mind if I cop a squat?"

"Not at all," I said breathlessly, not slackening my pace.

"You've had quite a workout." Carly said through a yawn. "Almost done?"

"Not yet," I panted, glancing at my watch. "About ten minutes more."

"Hmm," she said, squinting her green eyes at me. "Think you could cut it short and come down to my room for a little while?"

"I suppose," I said, breaking my rhythm and bending over to catch my breath. "Please tell me . . . you have water . . . in your fridge."

Carly stood. "I have water *and* Diet Coke in my fridge!"

"You are my hero," I said, trailing her, my feet aching with every step.

I hadn't been in her room, and a dorm room seemed odd with only one bed. In the extra space, she had two oversized purple beanbags squished against the wall. Above her bed were posters of butterflies. Carly grabbed two cans of Diet Coke out of her tiny refrigerator and handed me one, sitting carefully on the edge of her bed, as though she were afraid to wrinkle the blankets. I thanked her, flopped wearily into one of her beanbags, still short of breath, and said, "So what's up?"

Carly took a slow sip, then set her drink carefully on her bedside table, precisely in the middle of the coaster. It troubled me that she seemed to be hesitating so long in answering back.

"Carly?" I probed. "Is everything okay?"

Carly scooted off her bed to the floor and sat across from me, Indian-style on her furry, lavender rug. "Sweetie," she said, "I think I know your secret."

"What secret?" I asked quickly.

"I see what's happening," she said, gesturing to my body. "Jena, it's not good."

"What's not good?" I asked, playing dumb. I twisted a section of the furry rug in my fingers.

Carly was silent a moment more. The weight of her gaze was almost too much to bear. Then she asked, "Are you one of the girls who has been throwing up?"

"What? No!" I said, honestly shocked. "I don't do that!"

"So you just don't eat? I haven't seen you in the dining hall since orientation when I met you. Ally is worried. She hasn't seen you eat anything in months."

I sighed. *Ally,* I thought. *I should have known.* "I do eat," I said. "Ally just isn't usually with me. I'm so busy we actually don't see one another very much."

"Well, something is wrong. You do have an eating disorder, whether you realize it or not." Carly moved to meet my eyes. "And the reason I can say that is because I struggle with one, too. I've been battling bulimia since high school."

"You have?" I asked in disbelief.

"Not many people know. I've been through treatment, and I've been doing really well. But it was a real battle to get to this point. I seriously needed help, and I got it." Carly drew in a sharp breath. "You need help, too."

I looked away. No one had yet dared to say the words "eating disorder" to me since middle school. I didn't appreciate having the diagnosis tossed into my lap by a fellow student. I was even more uncomfortable because she was right.

———————

A Friday night in March, snow beginning to surrender to spring's first warm rousing breath. It should have been an incredible evening—a night of music and friends and laughter and lights. I was part of a band called "Six Lunatics," whose repertoire mostly included covers of hits by the popular 1980s political rock band 10,000 Maniacs, and we were overjoyed to be playing a gig—a nonpaying gig, save for tips, but no matter—at a coffee and juice bar in downtown Naperville. The atmosphere was unabashedly collegiate, a bookworm chic more contrived than casual. The menu included wheat grass smoothies and soy lattes and a signature blended vegetable drink called Oxygen. Students filled the tiny storefront cafe, wearing torn jeans and Birkenstocks and hemp ponchos, nodding in and out of time with our upbeat tempos, mouthing the words of songs they knew.

I was having a ball, flitting giddily between keyboard and drum kit and the center stage mic, swapping lead and backing vocals with a girl named Shawn. My friends were at three small tables in front, and it was thrilling to see them singing along, signaling approval with enthusiastic tapping of fingers and toes.

I should have heeded the warning signs—the tunnel vision, the clammy forehead, the pins-and-needles sensation in my hands and feet. I should have sat out a few numbers, maybe even had a few gulps of wheat grass myself. Woulda, coulda, shoulda. Instead, I played on, the metaphorical Energizer Bunny banging the drum on . . . and on . . . and on . . .

Blackness.

A loud bang, then throbbing and muffled sounds fading in and out.

I had gone limp, dropped my microphone, and slid off of my stool, hitting my head on the corner of a monitor. Somebody called the paramedics, but by the time they arrived I had come to, and I refused to be taken to the hospital. They questioned me endlessly about possible symptoms I may have been experiencing, but I assured them I had none, lying through my teeth about the ones I did have—dizziness upon standing, ringing in my ears, nausea. One of them asked if I knew whether or not I was hypoglycemic. I started to say no, but Ally called out from behind me, "She never eats."

"Shut up, Al," I snapped, surprised at my own tone. "I probably just got too hot. I'm fine now—really."

I sat out the last set and reluctantly consented to drink a glass of juice as I listened to Shawn sing lead on one of my favorite songs, ironically entitled "How You've Grown."

I had sung the song as my senior solo at my last high school choir concert. With two of my dearest friends accompanying me on piano and cello, I had sung the lyrics as homage to what we were leaving behind: childhood and innocence and security. My friends and teachers had cried, touched by the beauty of the song. This time, listening with my head throbbing and my stomach still queasy, it was I who sat with tears streaming as I realized how homesick I was for my high school friends and for the euphoria I had known during those years.

As deeply in denial as I was about the severity of my eating disorder, on some level I had a real-time sense that I was blowing it. I was allowing myself to sink deeper and deeper into an illness so all-consuming it would have power to draw me away from all I claimed to be working toward. In one sense, I was chickening out, drifting carelessly toward death as a sleepy, gutless alternative to what would have been far more courageous a choice: life.

Soon after my humiliating collapse at the coffee house gig, a favorite professor approached me as I passed by his office in Pfeiffer Hall on my way to a rehearsal.

"Jena, you sweet thing," Dr. Menendez called after me in his charming Costa Rican accent. "Let me talk to you for a moment, will you?"

I smiled and backed up a few paces into his office. Known to the music students as Pete (not his real name, but no one asked questions), Dr. Menendez always referred to me as "you sweet thing" because that was his way of referring to *everyone*. Still, he had a way of making me feel special nonetheless.

"Yes?" I asked, figuring he wanted to tease me about something, as always.

"Let me look at you, you silly one," Pete said, walking in a complete circle around me. "Tell me what has happened to you."

"What? Nothing has happened to me, that I know of," I replied, still waiting for the punchline.

"You sweet, sweet thing, you have absolutely no rear end whatsoever."

I laughed at the silliness of his words, exacerbated by his humorous accent and manner of speaking. "Hey, don't you be looking at my rear end!"

"I'm not looking at it, I'm looking *for* it!" Pete said, still circling me. "Jena, my dear one, there is just nothing *left* to you. Tell me what is going on."

"Pete! You're freaking me out. Nothing is going on. I've got this under control."

"Don't tell me you've got it controlled. I see you every morning in my class, seven a.m., drinking your silly Diet Coke," he said, which I found funny for some reason. "It makes me sad, because you're the only student in this crazy department that I like. The rest of them are imbeciles. They're hopeless. You cannot die and leave me here alone with these morons."

I laughed again. He was joking, but I sensed the genuine worry. He cared.

"I'm not going anywhere, Pete," I smiled, patting him on the arm.

"You know, there's a student counseling center in Old Main. They're morons, too, I'm sure, but they might be helpful morons. You should talk to them and see if they can help you."

"Would that make you feel better?" I asked playfully.

"It would, it really would," Pete said, through his trademark exaggerated ear-to-ear grin. "Do it for me, the only prof you really like. I'm your favorite—I know I am. You cannot hide your feelings for me. Do it for your favorite person in this whole school."

"Aarrghh," I moaned, consenting. "How can I argue with that?"

The student counseling center in Old Main—the oldest building on campus, tall, yellow-stoned, and stately—was essentially two little rooms, a few ratty, gold fabric chairs that had seen better days, a coffee pot, a metal desk, a few houseplants on their way out, and a couple of social workers thrown in for good measure. The place smelled like weak coffee and nondairy creamer and the ghosts of professors from ages past who must have smoked in the classrooms with the windows tightly shut.

The person I spoke with was middle-aged, kind and mild-mannered, and a little distracted on that particular day by something outside the window behind my head. I don't recall her name. I'm not even sure she was a social worker; she may have been a counselor with some other designation, or a semiretired psych nurse or just someone who liked to listen to people's problems, like a bartender. I remember only incoherent snippets of that conversation, something along the lines of:

"And you're having trouble with . . . ?"

"I've lost a little weight recently."

"And by a little weight, you mean . . . ?"

"About forty pounds."

"And this weight loss started . . . ?"

"A few months ago."

"And you're not doing drugs?"

"No."

"Do you want to stop losing weight?"

"No."

"Do you feel you are too thin?"

"No."

"Do you intend to eat dinner after you leave here?"

"No."

Time passed, the clock ticking away in loud rhythmic clicks. She asked, half-listening, her eyes flitting to the nameless thing outside the window and back to me. I got the impression that I was boring her or that she was becoming more and more aware of what she was missing on TV. I also got the impression that she saw this sort of thing all the time—bony, sullen girls sitting in front of her, whining and crying and bouncing their knees. Her job, I gathered, was to sort us out and hand out the appropriate business cards.

I must have been easy to classify because I was out in forty-five minutes, shuffling away from Old Main in the crisp, chilly air with two therapists' business cards, along with a brochure about the dangers of eating disorders. I remember walking slowly down the sidewalk, reading the brochure and feeling a mixed-grill of emotions: shame (I was a sick person, after all—a head case, totally mental, in a clinical sense), guilt (this was not what I was at school for; I was wasting time, wasting energy, wasting good scholarship money), and excitement (because I knew, deep down, that I had gone away to school with a strong, morbid desire to self-destruct, and by golly, it was working).

I sat in my car, still holding the brochure and the cards, and unwrapped a piece of Trident, writing the number five in my notebook. I had begun to record my *gum* calories. I thought how petty and stupid it was to do this. Then I got distracted by my thighs, which were squished against the driver's seat, and tried to imagine them after I'd lost another twenty pounds, when there would be far less to squish. I tore up the cards and brochure and sped off, my jaw set like flint.

CHAPTER 6

*I*n the early days, when starvation was still romantic and exciting, there were occasions when I found myself behaving in ways completely outside of my natural character and constitution. Call it a high, call it garden-variety self-destruction, call it an unprecedented phase of overdue teenage rebellion. But by spring, now under the one-hundred-pound mark, I began at times to experience life in the third person, as though I were playing a two-dimensional character not me at all, so therefore I had no personal responsibility. The real Jena was somewhere in limbo, in a holding pattern, while my shell (or my skeleton?) was free to experiment, to go a little crazy, to test the choppy waters of uncharted territory.

A group of students had conspired to take me up to Chicago for a night on the club circuit, convinced I was a classic stress-case in need of "party therapy." In their well-meaning collegiate minds, an eating disorder was nothing a little booze and some strobe lights couldn't fix.

We drove into the city in an old black Chrysler LeBaron convertible, with a sophomore we all knew as Lodi at the wheel. The air was cool, but someone insisted we put the top down. So we drove north along I-55, wind whipping our hair, drunk with freedom. Halfway there, I was so cold my lips were blue; one by one my friends took off their coats and sweatshirts, layering me up in the backseat.

I both relished and resented the attention. This sort of dichotomy is inherent to those with eating disorders. We are at once introverted and extroverted, both wanting to hide and to be seen, especially once we have begun to take on that curious pallor of the half-dead. It is not uncommon for an anoretic to hide herself under layers and layers of clothing one day and to wear as little as possible the next day, bounding around in size-zero jeans and a camisole, flaunting her bones.

We finally ended up at some smoky nightclub on Halsted and sneaked in under the bouncer's radar, all of us underage. It was decidedly not my scene, twentysomethings grinding to the relentless dance beat of house music, colored lights flashing on hot, wet skin as bodies moved like jellyfish over the old parquet dance floor, cocktails in hand.

I took off my coat, laid it over the bar-height table, and turned to find Lodi handing me an orange-colored drink with a cherry and umbrella. "Try it, you'll like it."

"What is it?" (My heart began to palpitate with fear: I hadn't thought about having to drink. How would I calculate the calories?)

"Amaretto Stone Sour. They're awesome."

He was waiting for me to drink. Trapped, I took a slow sip, trying to fake my way through. To my surprise, my tongue thrilled to the sweet-and-sour mixture of orange juice and alcohol. I hadn't had anything to drink besides lemon water and Diet Coke for months.

"Good, huh?" Lodi smiled, beginning to dance. I nodded and took another sip, deciding to allow myself to nurse exactly one half of the drink throughout the evening. It seemed like a safe plan, considering I had only eaten two apples all day and it was approaching ten o'clock.

Note: If you ever want to get someone drunk, pour three ounces of alcohol into the empty stomach and underweight frame of a Christian girl who has never had a drink in her life, then stand back and watch.

It hit me quickly. Within an hour I was doing the Electric Slide with Lodi, Kim, Mandy, and Dave. When the song ended, I felt a hand on my waist and turned to face a handsome twenty-ish guy with wire-rimmed glasses and sandy hair cut in that mid-90s skater style, falling over one eye.

"Hey, Tiny," he said flirtatiously. "Wanna dance? I was watching you out there; I know you know how." He was grinning impishly, but he seemed harmless.

"Dance . . . with you? Oh, um, well . . ." I shot a glance to Mandy, who waved me, her mischievous brown eyes admonishing me to live a little.

"I won't bite," the skater boy probed. "Just one dance."

"One dance—what the heck," I agreed, my usual inhibitions diluted by the atmosphere and alcohol.

He was a good dancer. Sometime during the three-minute song, he introduced himself as Troy, a theater student at DePaul University.

"So you must be a dance student, right?" he asked. "Ballet, I'm guessing. You have a dancer's body."

"You couldn't be more wrong," I laughed, but I felt vindicated. After months of being called a skeleton by my friends, I now knew they had been overdramatizing. I didn't look sick—I looked like a *dancer,* a description I would tuck away and use later to prove my thesis that I was entirely healthy.

The night wore on, and everyone grew drunk. Troy asked me to come home with him, wherever home was. And here's what floors me, recalling the evening: I was all set to take him up on it. Maybe it was because I was drunk for the first time and delirious from starvation to boot. Maybe it was because tossing the body around like a used rag seemed like an appealing new form of self-destruction to add to my growing arsenal of abusive practices. Or maybe it was just because he had called me thin.

"Are you crazy?" Mandy asked, when I told her I was leaving with a total stranger. "You could get yourself raped!"

"Well, I'm letting loose," I slurred, growing dizzier.

Lodi slipped his arm around my waist. "Come on, kiddo, we're taking you home."

I found this hilarious, for some reason. "Are you gonna carry me? Lodi, no, you'll throw your back out!"

Lodi scooped me up in his skinny college boy arms and said, "Whatever! You weigh like fifty pounds."

It disturbs me now to remember how pleased I was, being told that I weighed next to nothing. I felt very strongly then that I could *never* go back. I had a desperate need to stay skinny, and I renewed my vow to do whatever it would take.

The Bible tells us that when Satan lies, he speaks his native language, because the truth is not in him. The truth *was*, however, in *me*: God's Spirit was in my heart. The problem was, I was not giving Him my *mind*. And without the revealing, life-giving words of God shining in the darkness of our minds, Satan's lies become easily believable.

I believed I needed—and deserved—to be sick, frail, weak. I had the sense that I had painted myself into a corner and could never escape. What truly disturbs me about the whole thing is that, trapped in that deadly corner, I thought I was *happy*.

———

Early spring, 1996. My weight had been hovering just above ninety pounds for months, and my family, having flipped out at the sight of me during winter break, had already had enough of waiting for me to "get over it." I was not getting over it; I was becoming even more intent on continuing my private disappearing act. Anorexia is an addictive behavior, and I had fallen, hook, line and sinker.

The addiction was manifold. There is the initial physiological response to starvation: the sharpness of one's senses, the palpable sense of power over the flesh and over the self, and the sneaking suspicion that you have become invincible. There is also the addiction one develops to the extreme thinness; for me, that particular addiction took over. After a lifetime of hypersensitivity to the amount of space I was occupying, it came as a relief to find myself taking up no more space than I had at the age of ten. I had always felt the world was a little too much for me, a bit too loud and glaring and menacing. But now that I didn't fit anymore—now that I had shrunken away from all that once contained me—I felt safer. I walked among these human beings, an impostor in their midst, but I wasn't really *there*.

I wasn't pulling myself through. It had become clear to those who loved me that I was not at all likely to do so on my own. So, after losing several arguments and battles of logic, I allowed myself to be coerced into meeting with some woman with some title from some organization I cannot recall for an eating disorder screening. I do not remember the woman's name—or her face or voice or much of anything she asked me.

I remember this: she diagnosed me, clinically and officially, with anorexia nervosa, restricting type. I learned there are specific diagnostic criteria that one must meet to receive such a clinical diagnosis: decrease in body weight of at least 15 percent, amenorrhea (loss of menses) lasting at least three consecutive months, the obvious disordered eating, and pathological weight fixation. I met all of the criteria. It was official. I had no defense. I had been found out.

And I was relieved—an unlikely reaction to being caught red-handed. I felt validated, perhaps because I had become so accustomed to *achievement* as a way of life that I viewed even my illness through such a lens: I was a *successful* anoretic.

Having been officially diagnosed, I was asked by everyone in my life to begin counseling. My little problem was no longer a secret, and although I did not see it, I wore its effects openly— on my wasted body, in my skittish movements, in my haunted eyes. No one was letting me off the hook anymore—not my professors, not my friends, and no one back home. I felt trapped and sat myself down to make a plan. The plan was simple: play along, go to therapy for a few weeks, humor everyone, and then crawl back into my hole, shrug shyly, and say, "I tried."

I figured everyone would calm down and eventually get over their keen awareness of my descent; all I had to do was wait them out. I had found comfort in sickness, had embraced it as a way of life rather than as a means toward death. And no one was going to take that away from me.

Pull Up a Couch

*I*t was a warm day in April when I arrived for my first session with Meg Estes at her Naperville clinic. I was shocked by the drop in temperature in the building; I hadn't expected air conditioning and hadn't brought a sweater. I sat on one of the sage green leather chairs in the waiting room, my wasted muscles stiffening against the cold. I turned my head to read the spines of books on the shelves across from me: *Father Hunger, When Food Is Foe, Fasting Girls, Reviving Ophelia.*

I picked up a tri-fold brochure from the table beside me: "Megan K. Estes, MA, LCPC. Meg holds a Masters Degree in Professional Counseling and is working on a doctorate degree, and has specialized in treating eating disorders for the past fourteen years."

Great, I thought, returning the brochure to its acrylic holder. I knew I would be seeing a counselor and would have to spill a few secrets eventually, but I hadn't prepared myself for an actual expert on eating disorders. Anorexia was a subject many counselors knew only minimally, and few were considered experts. I hadn't counted on coming across an "expert" right in my college town.

"Jena?" Meg's voice startled me out of my reverie.

"Yep," I answered, standing too quickly.

"Come on back," Meg said, smiling. I trailed behind her, hyperconscious of my new surroundings: dimly lit office, lots of potted plants, monstrous fluffy beige couch, bookshelves along three walls, mahogany desk on an angle, coffee table with coasters and Kleenex, the conspicuous smells of lavender potpourri and tea.

I settled into the huge couch, pulling a pillow onto my lap as a shield, and inspected Meg: short, highlighted blond hair curled into a sporty flip and tucked behind her ears, with three tiny diamond stud earrings, impossibly white teeth, charcoal gray pencil skirt, black hose and heels, French blue poplin shirt with a stiff white collar and cuffs, silver Tiffany choker necklace, and a rather substantial princess-cut diamond on her left hand. Were it not for her extremely soft-spoken demeanor, which gave her away as a therapist, I might have expected her to invite me into her sleek BMW and show me million-dollar condos on the North Shore.

"What made you decide to come in for help?" Meg asked in her near-whisper.

"Well, a lot of people have been sort of on me for a while to talk to someone, and I . . . guess I ran out of excuses not to." I shrugged.

"That's as good a reason as any," Meg said with a smile, jotting notes on her clipboard. "Do you agree with them that you need help in managing your eating disorder?"

"Sometimes."

"Sometimes you need help, or sometimes you agree with them?"

"The second one," I replied, suddenly confused.

"What makes you feel you need help? How is your eating disorder disrupting your life?"

"Um . . . well, I guess it keeps me from enjoying where I am in my life right now. I'm a little distracted."

"Distracted from what?"

"From school and friends . . . from what I need to be learning, I guess."

"Do you find it hard to concentrate in class?"

"Yes," I admitted. "I'm finding it hard to concentrate right now."

Meg looked up and smiled. "I know you are. That is usually what finally brings a person in for treatment. It's frustrating when you can't think anymore. How about physically? Any symptoms I should know about?"

"A little dizziness," I said, trying to sound casual.

"Seeing spots when you first stand up?" I nodded, growing nervous. I didn't want to share *too* much. "And what is your food intake now? How many calories per day?"

"Three hundred."

"Do you binge?"

"No. I'm terrified at the very thought," I said. "I have nightmares about it."

"Do you know what your weight is currently?"

"Yes," I answered, volunteering nothing further.

"And what is your weight?" Meg persisted.

"Um," I stalled. "About a hundred and five, last week when I checked."

"You weighed one-o-five last week? I find that hard to believe."

"Why?" I laughed nervously.

"Because if that's the case, you've dropped considerable weight in the past week."

"Hmm," I said, feeling guilty for lying. "Maybe."

"We actually won't be focusing so much on weight and numbers as we continue to meet, if we do in fact decide to meet regularly," Meg said. "But we need a starting point, so I'd like to have you weigh in now with me."

"You actually have a scale here?"

"No, but the dietitian I work with is right across the hall, and we have a medical scale in her office." Meg addressed me firmly: "It's important that I know your weight today, Jena. Are you okay with that?"

"You don't make it sound like I have a choice."

"No, you do have a choice. You can choose not to work with me. But if you would like to continue seeing me for a while, I will need you to weigh in."

I was silent a few moments, trying to calculate the risk verses the benefit. I knew I couldn't simply opt out of seeing Meg already; how would I silence my critics? Feeling trapped, I reluctantly followed her into Kim Bergen's office across the hall.

"Okay, Jena, kick your shoes off and hop on up," Meg instructed me as my knees began to tremble, both from fear and from cold. I stepped onto the chilly metal platform and bit my lip while Meg slid the weight across the bar, down, down, down. "You're at about ninety-one pounds today."

"Ninety-one?" I echoed, unable to disguise my pleasure.

"Yep," Meg answered, recording the number in her notes. "Let's head back and we'll talk a bit more about what that means."

Again I trailed behind, slightly apprehensive. Did she have the power to hospitalize me? My panic subsided quickly, calmed by the consolation prize of another pound lost.

"Okay," Meg began as we returned to her cozy office. "So what does it mean to you that you weigh ninety-one pounds right now?"

"It's less than I thought, I guess."

"And are you relieved? Happy? Scared?"

I wavered. Was there a right answer? "All of the above, I guess."

"What scares you about weighing ninety-one?"

"Nothing. I'm more scared about what you will say it means. Do I have to go into the hospital?"

"You're nineteen. You're an adult. You don't have to do anything you don't want to do," Meg said.

"Oh," I replied, relieved. "Good."

"Do you intend to lose more weight?"

"Maybe," I said. I had nothing to lose by being honest, since she couldn't lock me away and force me to eat.

"Well, thank you for being honest," Meg said. "Obviously, though, I'm going to remind you that you are already very much underweight, and you would be putting yourself at even greater risk if you were to continue losing."

"I don't care."

"You don't care if you die?"

"I don't know," I admitted. "I mean, it's not like I'm suicidal or anything."

"Are you sure?"

"I'm sure. I don't want to kill myself. I'm not *trying* to die."

"What are you trying to do?"

"I'm just trying to . . . live."

"And having an eating disorder makes life easier?"

"Yes," I replied. "Somehow it does, even though I'm sure that doesn't make sense."

"It makes perfect sense, actually," Meg said. "I get it."

"Well, I'm glad you understand it, because I sure don't," I laughed nervously. "I just know I have to do it. I don't want to stop. I *can't* stop."

"I'm not even asking you to stop right now," Meg said. "I would be foolish to think you could. If you could stop, without being scared, you would. But you can't. So part of my job is to protect you from yourself as much as possible, so we can keep you around long enough to work *through* the fear so you *can* get well."

"How do you plan to do that?" I asked doubtfully.

"Well, you and I are going to draw up a contract," she began, "a contract regarding your treatment plan: what I agree to do and not to do, and what you agree to do and not to do. For example, I agree to be committed to you wholly during our sessions, and I agree to keep absolutely everything you share with me in the strictest confidence. This will be a safe place for you, if you choose to use it."

"What if my mom calls? Will you tell her anything?"

"Not unless you ask me to in advance."

I exhaled, somewhat relieved. "Okay."

"Also, I agree to respect our scheduled times together, to be here on time and prepared for the session, and I would ask the same of you," Meg relayed. "One more thing: you and I need to agree on a limit to the weight loss. We're going to decide on a number you agree not to fall below."

"Or else what?" I interjected quickly.

"Or else you will consent to be admitted into the hospital either for short-term refeeding or for an inpatient program."

"That seems drastic," I protested, unable to disguise my disapproval.

"Desperate times call for desperate measures," Meg retorted kindly. "Your disorder could kill you. Anorexia nervosa has the highest mortality rate of all psychological illnesses. People *do* die from this, Jena."

"But I'm not that skinny."

"Not as skinny as some and far skinnier than others, but that is irrelevant. I've worked with girls who weighed sixty pounds and girls who weighed a hundred and sixty. *All* of them had eating disorders, though, and so *all* of them were putting their lives at risk. Period."

"Hmm," I answered, unconvinced. "So what is this number?"

"What would be a fair weight you would be willing to agree not to go below?"

I pondered a moment and finally answered, "Eighty."

"Try again," Meg smiled.

"Eighty-one?"

"I say eighty-nine," Meg offered. "And no less."

"That's only two more pounds," I complained. "I could lose that much this week."

"I'm sure you could. But that would be your choice. The idea is not to give you a new goal weight you have to get to by next week. I'm giving you a two-pound margin for error, so to speak— to keep you *out* of the hospital. I think that's fair, don't you?"

I pouted a moment, pondering Meg's proposition. "I thought you said we wouldn't be talking any more about numbers."

"And we won't," Meg affirmed, "after today. But we have to have boundaries; in this case, they are for your physical protection more than your emotional protection. Because I understand how your disorder tends to progress, I would be irresponsible if I did not set these boundaries with you from the outset. Can you understand that?"

I shrugged. "I guess."

"Good enough," Meg said, winking at me. "Let's ink this deal."

Wading Deeper

$\mathcal{A}$s part of my treatment contract, I agreed to attend weekly support group meetings at a local behavioral health hospital, sponsored by an organization called ANAD (Anorexia Nervosa and Associated Disorders). Unbeknownst to me, my mother and a friend had previewed a meeting, and they offered to come along to my first one.

The meeting was horrible. The group was large, maybe thirty or forty sick people plus their supportive others, all perched precariously on chairs in a giant circle. They all introduced themselves: "I'm Jamie and I'm anorexic" or "I'm John and I'm a bulimic and an alcoholic" or "I'm Elizabeth and I'm a bulimarexic compulsive liar and gambler and shoplifter, as well as a sex addict." Their two-line bios were enough to make mine seem like a fairy tale in comparison, and it seemed to me I was the fattest person in the room—or at least the most normal-looking.

Suddenly, it was my turn. I glanced nervously at Gail, the group leader, who was peering at me hopefully, like a mother waiting for her toddler to take her first step. I drew in a sharp breath and said, "I'm Jena, and supposedly I have anorexia."

There were a few snickers, mostly from the inpatients, who glanced at one another knowingly, and then back at me, bemused. Gail allowed herself a wry smirk. "Supposedly?"

"Well, yeah, I mean . . . What I mean is . . ."

"That people around you are telling you that you have a problem," Gail said. "And you don't believe them, and you think maybe they're being overly dramatic?"

I shot Gail a dirty look and quickly regretted it. "Yes."

"Is it possible, Jena, that your friends and family are able to see you more clearly right now, more objectively, than you are able to see yourself? Because I've run this group for a long time," Gail said, "and I see people with eating disorders every day. I met your mom last week when she shared some of your story, and now that I'm meeting you, I have to say there is no doubt in my mind that you are, in fact, sick, and that you do, in fact, need help."

I decided then and there that I did not particularly like this Gail person. She was cocky, and she seemed to think she knew me after five minutes in my presence. To be fair, I also didn't like the others in the group, either—especially those who snickered and told me with their eyes that they had my number. (I should probably mention I was becoming quite paranoid at this stage in my illness.) I wanted to bolt. I wanted to kick my chair across the room as I left, flip them off—all of them—speed-walk to my car, and peel out of the parking lot, screeching my tires.

But I had a contract with Meg, an obligation. And I was a good girl.

———

One night when I visited the ladies' room during an ANAD meeting, it suddenly occurred to me that I was consciously choosing to proceed with my illness. Alone in the bathroom, I moved in slow motion, my thoughts thick as molasses as I surveyed my pasty reflection in the mirror above the sink. The details of my surroundings suddenly became intense— the garish florescence of the lighting on my cyanotic skin, the extremely cold air-conditioning, and the obnoxious, antiseptic smell of the hospital, all of which seemed to say: *Sickness*.

Deliberately, I took a seat on a mauve upholstered armchair and fixed my eyes blankly on one of the tiny one-inch-square floor tiles, thinking, *Is this what I want? Do I really want this? This* was illness and all that comes with the package: hospitals, medication, endless psychobabble, conversations peppered with new words such as *triangulation . . . transference . . . enmeshment . . . self-sabotage*. *This* was needles and labs and pills and nurses in scrubs, standing over me with orange juice and expressions of pity. I stood at the threshold of a whole new world, with new protocol and new vernacular. I was being invited to join a sub-society, a members-only club of sick people, with its own set of unspoken rules. The voice in my head shifted from first person to second: *Are you in, or are you out?* And as I stood slowly—very slowly, so as not to faint—and walked back toward a conference room full of sulking skeletons, I was wordlessly answering: *I'm in*. I was going to continue playing the role of someone who appeared to be addressing her illness, but I was consciouly deciding to remain sick. I was choosing to live a lie.

This is important to note: I made a choice. So often we see those who struggle with eating disorders and other addictions as hapless victims, unable to change. The Twelve Steps of Alcoholics Anonymous mandates that sufferers admit their powerlessness over the disease and surrender their will to a higher power. This step is often misinterpreted to mean that the sufferer is one-hundred-percent victim, in no way responsible. Although circumstances may have contributed to my descent into anorexia, I knew good and well that I had the ability—at least at this early stage—to make the right choice. I, for my own twisted reasons, simply chose otherwise. I purposely chose, and, never one to do anything lightly, I followed through with fierce determination.

I chose to be both "in treatment" *and* sick. Unfortunately, this is a popular choice among those with eating disorders, because we have opposing desires. We are people-pleasers who want to keep everyone happy (which means staying in treatment), but we are also gripped by an intense compulsion to hang on to our disorder as a maladaptive coping mechanism.

I took a temporary leave from school in April for what I thought would be just a few weeks. I needed a breather, I said. The truth was, I could no longer think, and I had to make a decision: stay and eat, or take a break and continue to starve. A person of reasonable emotional health might read this and wonder: Why would anyone *choose* sickness? What could possibly be tempting about mental illness, or slow and painful starvation, or an interruption of the normal life of a teenage girl? And still others—others like myself—might read this and say: Ah, yes.

To this day I do not fully understand the magnetic pull of this disorder—or of other forms of self-destruction. Was my break from college a cop-out, a way of escaping the pressures of studies and impending adulthood? Maybe. But if that was the case, it was certainly not the whole of it.

There is a part of us human beings that is simply rather dark and disturbed and maybe even a little morbid. It is the part we like to pretend isn't there or the part we crucified when we gave our hearts to Jesus and therefore it is no longer a problem, or maybe we even pretend we never had such a dark side to contend with at all. Maybe for many it simply has never caused such a struggle as it has for others. Maybe it lies dormant, and only when we fool with death on purpose do we fully awaken this brooding, evil curiosity about our own limits, our own mortality.

I know this: the longer and deeper I waded into the murky waters of death and self-destruction, the stronger that curiosity became until it was no longer curiosity but compulsion. My instinct toward life and safety became inverted, and eventually I began to lean more toward death as a default setting.

For a Christian, this is shameful. Such upheaval of the instinct to live is not the sort of thing you casually bring up as a prayer request at Sunday meeting. Rather it is something to keep tightly under wraps, hidden expertly behind a convincing smile and just the right amount of Christian jargon.

I wonder how many believers struggle in silence with taboo challenges—mental illness, addiction, obsessive thinking— because we wonder how we might be judged as followers of Christ. This must be heartbreaking to God, who longs to restore us and make us whole and whose love for us is big enough to withstand our ugliest secrets, none of which we could ever hide from His eyes, anyway.

The onslaught of concern from friends and family once you have begun to deteriorate seriously can be alienating and confounding, given the fact that you, the sufferer, have no capacity for seeing the reality they see. Your eyes simply do not work anymore. You see yourself, indeed, "through a glass dimly"—and that image grows dimmer with each passing day and with each pound lost.

Their concern seems, to you, a bit melodramatic. They plead with you to believe them when they tell you that you are dying, that you cannot go on this way, that you must find your way back before it is too late. Part of you wants to believe them, but the other part of you—the part that has taken the oars and paddled your leaky dinghy into these deadly waters—will not let you believe and will not let you see.

Still, there are nights when you lie in bed at two o'clock in the morning, glassy eyes transfixed on the happy moon outside your bedroom window and admit in that lonely hour that just maybe you really are on your way out. You sense it in the ache of your bones, the shallowness of your breathing, the flutter of your heart as it labors to pump blood throughout your wasted body with half the number of beats per minute that it once took to complete the task.

These are the nights when you admit you have two alternatives: you can recover, or you can accept the fact that your young life is likely playing out its final, anticlimactic chapter. Trouble is, for you, to recover is simply unthinkable, neither possible nor attainable. Recovery seems an intangible, faceless ghost you cannot grasp or behold—something that sounds good in theory but won't stand still long enough to give you a close look at it.

So, with a small measure of uneasiness, you resign yourself to the ultimate option. You lie there, exhausted and mute, trying to identify the emotion that envelops you as you realize you are dying. This isn't how you had planned things, but you no longer have the emotional energy to feel remorse properly. Silently, you apologize to God, because it feels like the thing to do.

Then you close your eyes and wait.

Meg discovered early that I am artistic, and she began implementing art therapy assignments. She asked me at the end of a session to draw a picture of myself "within my world." She wanted to see how the pieces of my life fit together and where I placed myself in relation to all of the pieces. Three days later, I brought in a colored pencil drawing of myself holding a conductor's baton, arms raised as if directing a choir. Beneath me in the drawing are jagged-edged puzzle pieces, all clustered together tightly. The pieces are colored different shades and labeled "Personal Ambitions: school, career, music, etc; Personal Relationships: friends, family, loved ones; Relations with Guys; Relationship to Myself: self-image, self-esteem, body image, self-love, self-respect." In the center puzzle piece, bright yellow, is written, "Relationship with GOD." Holding up the entire collage of jagged pieces are two male hands, upturned, as if to cradle it all gently but surely.

"Hmm," Meg said, holding the drawing. "Okay. Can you explain this to me?"

"Well," I began, "that's me at the top, with the baton. All the puzzle pieces are the different elements in my life or whatever, and God is in the middle because I really try to let everything else revolve around Him. Those are His hands, holding everything together."

"Mmm," Meg said. "So God is holding you up and holding everything together for you, which is a lovely thought. But this tells me that you expect God or somebody to hold you and not let you fall, yet you want to be the one holding the baton. You're in control, calling all the shots, while counting on God to make sure nothing falls to pieces."

"So?"

"Well, you can't have it both ways. Either you take charge of your life, like that strong woman holding the baton at the top of the drawing, or you drop the baton and give up control to your God and hope she's really out there to keep you from falling."

"She?" I asked, unfamiliar with hearing God referred to as female.

"Whoever you're calling God. To me, if there is a God, she

is female."

"Oh. Well, when I say God, I mean the God of the Bible," I said. "Jesus."

"Ah," Meg said, with a fleeting smirk. "So how long have you called yourself a Christian?"

"Since I was fifteen."

"Mmm." Meg was silent a moment. This infuriated me.

"*What?* Is that bad or something?" I asked, feeling my face growing red. "Do you think I'm stupid or naïve or something?"

"Of course not," Meg whispered. I hated it when she whispered. There is no discernible tone to a whisper. "Quite the contrary."

"So why do I get the feeling you don't approve of my faith?"

"I haven't said I don't approve of your faith, Jena," Meg said. "The truth is, I am concerned with your mental and emotional health, and because of your disorder, with your physical health. Your spiritual health is not my concern. We won't be dealing with that. I am a therapist, not a pastor or priest or spiritual adviser. I have nothing to offer you with regard to spiritual direction, but I have much to offer with regard to your mental health, which is what is compromised by your anorexia."

"So I can't talk about God here?"

"You can talk about whatever you'd like with regard to your illness. It is far more important that we talk about your personal choices and responsibility for your own wellness. Your recovery is not up to God or anyone else. It is up to you."

"I know that," I said, letting my irritation bleed through my tone. "But while I do the work, I can still trust my God to protect me and hold me up."

"Well, if she does exist, let's hope she holds you up."

"So you don't believe in God?"

"I believe we are responsible for our choices and our actions, and we choose our own destiny. You have the power to choose life or death, by either embracing or fighting this disorder. If you choose life, my job is to come alongside and train you to fight the illness so that you can live."

"But you don't believe in God," I repeated.

"No, Jena," Meg said and sighed. "But I believe in you, and in me, and I know we can beat this thing and you can recover. That is our goal."

"But if we can't rely on God to help guide us, where do you place your hope?"

Meg smiled. "My hope is in you, Jena." I'm sure she meant this to be empowering.

I laughed. "Meg?"

"Yes."

"We're doomed."

In Meg We Trust

I moved off campus for good on a Thursday in May, believing I would soon be back to make up forfeited credits and start again. I had no idea what awaited me.

I moved back into my bedroom in my mom's house, feeling like a complete failure. I continued to see Meg three times a week, and Kim, the dietitian, once a week (completely ignoring her prescribed dietary plan). I "temporarily" quit my job at the Gap at the suggestion of both my therapist and my store manager, who was possibly worried about the liability involved if I should drop dead on her sales floor.

Others saw me as being on sabbatical—taking a break to get my head screwed on straight. I saw myself as a college dropout, a quitter who had taken sickness to full-time career status. *Way to go, Screwup.*

In the distorted reasoning of my convoluted mind, I felt pressure to become as sick as possible. It was no good taking time off just to be *moderately* sick. The starving and the exercising alone would no longer suffice.

I became a gobbler of pills, any pills I could get my hands on, prescription and over-the-counter. My grandmother was put on a new drug for her Alzheimer's disease that caused her to lose her appetite completely, so the doctors switched her to a different medication. Knowing she would no longer need the old meds, I shamelessly swiped the vial, adding the pills to my daily ration of chemicals. *Fat cow, greedy thief.*

I began taking the dog's thyroid medication, handfuls of little blue tablets throughout the day. I called in to several area veterinarians, scheduling refills at staggered times of the month, so no one would become suspicious as I drove to and fro to keep my stash supplied.

The drugs, in combination with caffeine pills and herbal speed, transformed me into an insomniac gray zombie, glassy-eyed and perpetually agitated, in constant motion. Meg referred me to a psychiatrist who prescribed Ambien to help me sleep. I soon discovered that if I took it and *didn't* go to bed, I would enjoy some very entertaining hallucinations. I looked forward to them each night ("Ooh! Fireworks . . . on my closet doors!"), but the fitful sleep that eventually followed was tormented by bizarre and terrifying nightmares.

My disorder had gone beyond finding the latest weight-loss drug or appetite suppressant. It was no longer just about creatively lowering the number on the scale. It had become an all-out attack on my body, myself. I had located the self-destruct button, and I relentlessly pushed it any way I could.

What have I got to lose?

It was one of the most dark and desperate seasons in my young life. But looking back, I know it was not hopeless and not inescapable. God was there, just as He always had been. I had an intimate, personal relationship with the Savior. But I had not yet learned how to rely on His strength in my weakness, His steadfastness in my wavering, His calm in my storm.

I was still that young woman portrayed in my drawing, holding the conductor's baton at the top of the page. I had gotten myself into a fine mess, and the only remedy I could see was to do more of the same, with greater intensity, until the story faded to black and was finally over.

Proverbs 14:12 says, "There is a way that seems right to man, but in the end it leads to death." Trusting in what I thought felt right, I careened full-speed-ahead toward death.

If I'd had a better understanding then of God's character (compassionate and gracious, slow to anger, abounding in love and faithfulness, according to Psalm 86:15), I might not have kicked and fought Him so hard. I felt I could trust Jesus with my soul but not with my life, and certainly not with my weight. I was as deluded and deceived as they come.

It would take the Savior of my soul to be the Savior of my destiny.

Meg quickly discovered just how entrenched I was in body image distortion. In her estimation, I had had the disorder for most of my life—certainly since that day in the car when I was three—and that I had simply managed to keep it dormant until my teen years, when I discovered the power to act it out.

"This has gone on long enough," Meg said as I walked into her office one day in our second month of therapy. "Today I am going to attempt to prove that you do not see yourself accurately."

She had tacked up a six-foot sheet of butcher paper on the wall of her office, and she asked me to draw a life-sized outline of how I perceived my body shape. After I was finished with my drawing, she would trace my actual body on the paper in red, to show me the difference between my perception and reality.

I trembled as I held the smelly black permanent marker, poised in front of the blank white paper. I was afraid on so many levels. I was afraid to reveal the horrible image I had held of myself for so many years. I was afraid I might misrepresent that image, and the experiment would be wasted. Most importantly, I was afraid my worst fears would be realized: that my drawing and Meg's tracing would overlap perfectly and no discrepancy would be found.

Reluctantly, I began to drag the marker along the paper, with a tentative, skipping *squeak-squeak*. Meg followed the trail of my marker with intense concentration, all soft eyes and furrowed brow as I outlined a stocky human image—wide through the hips and thighs, squat and round and apparently built to last through a famine.

"Now stand back here by me and let's look at her," Meg instructed. I liked that she referred to my drawing in the third person, as though she were not me. I liked the notion that the image could be anyone other than me, anything other than the ugly truth. Meg continued, "What do you see?"

I shook my head in disgust. "She's completely out of proportion. Her hips are too wide. Her legs are too short, especially from knee to ankle. Her shoulders are narrower than her hips, so her hips look even bigger by comparison."

"Interestingly, though," Meg observed, "her arms are like little noodles."

I blushed. "I kind of like my arms, actually."

"I mean, she looks like she wouldn't be able to lift anything at all," Meg continued. "I'd never expect someone with arms like that to be able to do anything. I wouldn't expect her to be able to handle any kind of weight or burden . . . in fact, I might even try to take her burdens *from* her, to offer her some help. Wouldn't you?"

"Maybe," I replied, wondering if I ought to feel insulted.

"I mean, when I see someone so weak and frail, I have compassion and feel concerned, don't you?" Meg kept her eyes focused straight ahead on my drawing as she continued. "It's kind of nice to know others are concerned about us sometimes, isn't it, Jena?"

"Oh no, I see where you're going with this. Look, it's not like that. I don't like having skinny arms because it makes people worry about me."

"Do you think it's wrong to want others to worry about you?"

"Of course it's wrong," I replied firmly. "It's selfish."

"What's selfish about wanting concern from the people who love us? Is it wrong to want attention?"

"Yes. I mean, no. I mean, I don't know. Just . . . it's . . . I don't know. It's . . . selfish. We shouldn't feel like we need other people to notice us all the time."

"But we can't always control what we feel, can we?" Meg retorted. "We can berate ourselves and beat ourselves up as soon as the feeling arises, but by then it's kind of too late, because the feeling is already there. You know, wanting to know that others care about us is part of the human condition, Jena. You'd have to be completely apathetic not to want that."

"Do you want that?"

"Sure I do! If I were sick today or had laryngitis, I would hope that you would ask me how I was feeling. If you didn't, I might feel you didn't care about my well-being. If I had a cast on my arm, I would want you to ask me how I broke it and if I was in pain. It's the same thing."

"I don't think so," I said.

"Let's come back to that. Right now, it's time for the moment of truth," Meg said, uncapping her red marker. "Let's get you traced."

I moaned. "Meg, I really don't want to do this." I positioned myself against the butcher paper, trembling as Meg began to trace my body.

"Stop shaking." Meg laughed, struggling to get the outline right.

"I'm nervous!"

Meg smiled, continuing to draw. "No kidding?" She finished with my feet and stepped back. "Okay," she said, "You ready? You'll be surprised, Jena."

I stepped away from the paper and stood beside Meg with my eyes closed. "I can't open my eyes."

"Yes, you can."

With that, my eyes shot open and focused on the black and red image before me. A smile bent my mouth before I could control it. Meg was right: I was far smaller than I had drawn myself.

"Well?" she asked. "What do you think? Is she what you expected to see?"

"Not at *all*," I said, smiling stupidly.

Meg took my shoulders in her warm hands and turned me to face her. "Jena, I was telling you the truth about your body. Do you see that now?"

"I . . . guess . . ." I stammered, turning my eyes back to the image, to be sure it hadn't changed.

"So you can trust me. If we are going to get anywhere at all, you have *got* to trust me. Because if you feel I am someone you can trust, you might be able to give up some of this control, at least around me. And that would be a start."

Meg asked me to describe how I felt about the exercise. I was relieved, but feeling scared as well. "This sort of proves that I'm crazy, doesn't it? I'm delusional. I see things that aren't really there. Not only do I see pretend fat—"

"I like 'phantom fat' myself," Meg interjected.

"Not only do I see 'phantom fat,' but I feel it, too. I *feel* like I am living inside a fat person's body. How crazy does that make me?"

Meg smiled with her eyes as she sipped her tea. "Crazy enough to need a little help, that's all."

"A little help? More like a complete overhaul!"

Meg set her cup down and laughed. "Well, then, it's a good thing we have time on our side."

I left Meg's office that day feeling I had made my first real progress since we'd started meeting. I had no intention of doing anything drastic—like eating dinner or flushing all my pills—but I felt I could trust Meg. Until that point, I had not been sure. It bothered me that she was not a Christian therapist, but I liked her. I decided to stick it out and really try to work with her. I was to see her again in four days, and I found myself almost looking forward to it.

And that, as it turned out, was my mistake.

W hen I arrived for our next session, I brought a little sign for Meg's office. It said, "Just take life one earth-shattering crisis at a time."

"I love it!" she said, smiling brightly. "Thanks, Jena. But . . ."

"You're welcome," I said, pulling her throw pillows over me on the couch, getting into position. "But what?"

She hesitated, scratching her neck and looking away. She let out a quiet laugh and started, "That sign might be a little ironic, actually."

"Uh oh," I said, smoothing back my hair. "Do we have an earth-shattering crisis to deal with today?"

Meg sighed.

"Oh, man," I said. "Just tell me. Are you admitting me? Did I break the contract?"

"No, no, no," Meg said. "Although I would still like to see you go into the hospital, when you decide you're ready. But that's not the crisis."

"So there *is* a crisis?"

Meg smiled at me with sadness in her gray eyes. "I'm so sorry, Jena. I'm afraid today will be our last session. I'm moving to Ohio."

"What? No. *No!* Sorry," I stammered. "But . . . *no*, Meg!" I started to cry, feeling more and more like an idiot as the clock ticked away its seconds and I stared at Meg in disbelief through my tears. "When? I mean, when do you leave?"

"I start my new job there next week. I'm so sorry."

"No! You can't! Sorry."

"Don't apologize. You're allowed to be upset."

"It's just that . . . I was just beginning to trust you," I sobbed. "Now what?"

"Well, you'll learn to trust someone else. But now you know that you *can* trust, Jena, and that's a big deal for you."

I was hardly consoled. "Well, can I write you? I mean, is that allowed?"

"I'm afraid not," Meg said quietly. "I'm sorry."

I stared at her purple pillow on my lap, watching my tears darken the fabric as they fell. And then, as suddenly as they had started, the tears dammed. Meg must have seen my expression change. "What are you feeling, Jena?"

"Why should I tell you?" I asked, making eye contact for a split second.

"You're angry with me," Meg said.

"Well, could you have given me a little more time? A week or so, to get used to the idea?"

"Well, I wasn't . . ."

"And what happened to 'it's a good thing time is on our side'? What was that some kind of joke?"

"*You* still have time, Jena. Your plan covers many more sessions. You can get a lot accomplished, if you commit to it," Meg said.

"With whom?"

"I've made a list of several therapists who accept your insurance."

"You want me to start *over?*"

"I don't believe you have any other choice, Jena. You need help."

"If we're done, I'm done. That's it."

"Mmm. That sounds a little manipulative to me, to be honest with you."

"Whatever."

"Well," Meg said, shifting in her chair, "if you don't want to continue in therapy, I think you only have one other option. And maybe this was meant to be, because I feel it is actually the better option."

"The hospital?"

"Not just any hospital, Jena. I'd like to see you go inpatient, in an eating disorder facility."

"I'm not sick enough for that," I retorted.

"Oh, yes, you are. Even if I weren't moving, I would be suggesting the same thing. I believe you need inpatient care to beat this." Meg looked at me long and hard before adding, "The sooner the better."

I shook my head.

"You're *worth* it, Jena," she whispered. "You deserve more of a life than this." She gestured toward my body. "This is no way to live. I wouldn't wish this on my worst enemy. You're miserable, you're in pain, you're tired, you're sick, you're cold. This is the last time I will ever see you, Jena. I want it to be because I'm moving, not because you're dying."

I sobbed quietly.

"If I could leave you a parting gift, it would be courage. I want to give you courage so you can take this necessary step for yourself. And if you'd like to give me a parting gift, what I'd like most is for you to agree to go inpatient."

I laughed through my tears. "That sounds a little manipulative to me, to be honest with you."

Meg winked, and tears stood in her eyes. "Whatever."

That was on a Friday. As I drove away from Meg's office for the last time I wept, remembering the look in her teary eyes. Her words reverberated in my brain, the way those echoing voice-overs play in movies: "This is no way to live . . . you're worth it . . . I give you the gift of courage . . ."

For a moment, I was inspired. I stopped at a coffee house and ordered my usual cafe americano of strong espresso and hot water. Just as the man behind the counter was telling me my total, a voice leapt out of the back of my throat and lunged forward, spewing, "And a blueberry muffin, please." I wanted to slap my hand over my mouth. Who had said that? Was that *me?*

"Sure thing," he said, and reached into the bakery case. I did the math in my head. Small muffin, probably not reduced-fat . . . Two hundred twenty calories, maybe ten grams of fat? Twelve? I stared at the white paper bag while the man rang up my new total. "Three thirty-nine," he said.

"What?"

"Three dollars and thirty-nine cents, please."

I must have stood mute for five full seconds, numbers flying around in my disorganized head. Numbers had begun to become a problem; I had begun to confuse numbers of calories and fat grams with numbers of dollars and cents, numbers of pounds, numbers of inches. In my brain, I registered that the barista had just told me the muffin contained 339 calories, and I was confused.

"Miss?" the man in the apron repeated. "That will be three-thirty-nine."

"Oh! Sorry," I stammered, handing over the sweaty wad of bills. I took the coffee and muffin and walked to my car, zombielike. I started the engine and cranked up the heat full blast, even though it was late June, letting the warm air run up the sleeves of my sweatshirt as I placed my hands over the vents on the dash. My teeth chattered. My lips and fingernails were blue. I felt like I might faint.

And I decided, quite casually, just to eat the stupid muffin.

I unwrapped it from its wax paper, watching it warily as if it might bite me. I lifted it to my face and smelled it. I picked off the tiny crumbs of sugar on the top and ate them one by one, granule by granule. I wanted, suddenly, to devour it—in one gigantic bite, the way a snake swallows a mouse. My stomach churned. My pulse quickened. My mouth watered.

Eat now, pay later, threatened the voice in my head. *Don't be a fool.*

"This is no way to live," Meg's voice echoed again.

What does she know? She's never known how amazing it feels to be this thin. Get rid of the muffin. Just do it, before you give in. Don't be weak!

I held the muffin to my lips, breathing in its sweet, buttery aroma. I had never wanted anything with such an intense desire in my life. It terrified me. I pinched off a tiny bite and put it in my mouth, and then I threw the rest out the driver's side window. As I put the car in drive and sped off, I thought, *Dear God. Help me.*

———

On the drive home, I thought about what inpatient treatment might be like. None of the images were pretty. I imagined the psych hospital where I went for weekly ANAD meetings. I pictured myself swaddled in blankets in a bed there, and Gail standing in my doorway gloating as nurses brought in trays of fattening food and held me down while I ate it. I imagined myself outgrowing my beloved child-sized clothes and hiding in sweatpants for the rest of my life, and visitors coming to see me week after week, each time finding me a bit larger than they had left me, and commenting on how much "better" I was looking.

At a stoplight, I reached into my backpack for my little orange laxative pills and popped fifteen out of their bubble pack, chugging them down in one gulp of warm coffee. Suddenly I felt as if I had grown a double chin, so I checked my face in the rear-view mirror and could have sworn I *saw* one as well, or at least the start of one. I reached back into my backpack and pulled out a sheet of blue diuretic tablets and a bottle of yellow caffeine capsules. I made myself a colorful handful of pill confetti and swallowed them all before the light turned green. *I'm sorry, God,* I thought. *Forgive me.*

That night, in my mother's living room, I lay on her couch shaking uncontrollably. I spiked a fever of 103 degrees and broke out in a cold sweat, my teeth chattering loudly. Mom covered me with one blanket, then another, then my coat, then a warm towel fresh from the dryer. Then she sat on the edge of the couch and cried. "What are we gonna do, Jen?" she implored, her brown eyes spilling desperate tears.

I told her what Meg had said about wanting me to go inpatient. I only brought it up because I hated to see my mom so scared and upset, and I wanted to provide her with an answer, to make it all better. For a moment, I wasn't thinking about myself or the horrible visions I'd had in the car.

Years later, Mom would tell me something that sent chills down my spine. The night before this fever happened, she had checked on me while I slept. Finding me uncovered in bed, she had realized how emaciated I had become. She covered me and went into her bedroom closet, where she fell on her face before God and surrendered me to His care. "If You have to take her home," she prayed, "take her home. I won't resent You for it." The very next night, I came home with the fever.

Mom agreed with Meg, and she brought out a brochure for an inpatient eating disorder treatment facility called Remuda

Ranch. It was a Christian facility; someone from church had given it to her weeks ago.

I lay there, buried under clothing and covers, shaking like a rabid animal. My stomach began to twist and cramp from all the pills, and my calves tightened into charley horses, a result of dehydration and depleted electrolytes. I listened as she read to me about the program: one-on-one therapy, art therapy, body image groups, relapse prevention, and her favorite, equine therapy, in which the patients each were assigned a horse to care for, ride, and groom. Under any other conditions, I would have dismissed the whole idea and run away to my room or my car, but I was in far too much pain to move. Besides, I suddenly remembered I had no therapist. The timing seemed right, even if nothing else did.

"Okay," I whispered, after she had finished.

"What?" she asked.

"I'll go," I said, squeezing my burning eyes shut, wincing in pain.

"You'll go?" Mom asked, brightening with hope.

"I'll go," I repeated. And then I passed out.

Bon Voyage

The admissions process to get me into Remuda is a blur. I remember phone interviews with members of the intake and admission staff, when I took the phone into my bedroom closet so as not to be overheard. I filled out surveys and inventories and applications for financial aid. I felt relieved that I would not be admitted for several weeks. I had time to starve, to get my weight as low as possible before they began refeeding me.

Three weeks without a therapist, without school friends trying to make me eat, with nothing to do but pack and concentrate on getting sicker. This is the part of the horror film where you might want to cover your eyes.

I began to deteriorate more quickly, and I felt it.

The mental slowness both malnutrition and dehydration induce is truly debilitating. Your responses are slowed, you search for words and names to no avail, you slip in and out of the present, losing ground and losing time.

Invincible as I thought I was, I was not immune to these effects. One day I spent nearly an hour standing on the stairs, lost in time, trapped mid-flight. I don't recall why I was headed up, but I had to stop on the sixth or seventh stair to rest because my emaciated, dehydrated body would not carry me up all fourteen in one trip. I stood, one foot on the riser in front of me, hand gripping the oak railing, staring absently through double vision at the cuff of my white sock, so loose on my birdlike ankle that the elastic gapped and folded instead of stretching, which pleased me.

After a few minutes, I probably could have made it the rest of the way to the second floor, but suddenly the whole process of climbing the stairs seemed so *complicated*. Which foot would I have to move first, the right or the left? It would have been much easier if the staircase hadn't had a tendency to tilt forward, to sway from side to side like a swinging bridge, to change colors—black, green, pink, black, green, pink.

I pressed my fists to my eyes and tried to focus. I waited for the black spots to stop flashing and glanced at my watch, making a mental note to poke yet another hole in the strap for a better fit. Fifty-five minutes had ticked away since I'd begun my journey up to my room.

My movements, my usually hyperactive gestures, my emotional responses all took on an odd sluggishness as my body began to consume itself for energy. This is different from atrophy; when muscles atrophy, they begin to wither from lack of use. When a genuine famine exists in the body, the body will cannibalize itself, actually eating itself away—first fat, then muscle, then organs. This explains why medical textbooks list "shrinkage of the brain" as an effect of starvation.

My brain was shrinking. I was, ounce by ounce, losing my mind.

July 24, 1996. The night before I left for Arizona, I headed out to do some last-minute shopping. I needed the things one might expect to need when being sent off to spend nearly a year in a psychiatric facility: a good bra, lotions and body sprays, and a bathing suit. One might have thought I was preparing for a cruise to Tahiti.

The truth was, I wanted a good bra to keep my chest under wraps, since I feared weight gain would cause me to pop out of my shirt in an instant, like an airbag deploying from the steering wheel on impact. I wanted lotions and sprays to keep me smelling like vanilla, which is comforting to me (however ironic it may be for a skeleton to smell like cake). The bathing suit was a dreaded necessity, called for in the "what to pack" section of the Remuda brochure; I saved that horrible purchase for last.

I stood in front of the full-length mirror in the fitting room at Old Navy, wearing a yellow-and-green plaid bikini. The suit was a size XS, and still the molded cups were empty against my bony chest, and the bottoms sagged in the butt, hanging like an empty pouch below my protruding coccyx, with two obnoxiously cheerful little bows adorning my naked pelvic bones.

I stared at my reflection. My legs were milky white, webbed with blue veins, and my feet were a ridiculous shade of purple. My upper arm was precisely half the width of my elbow, and my thighs were no wider than my knees, all the way up. My face was scariest of all: gray with sunken eyes and cheeks, and a big, blue vein bulging and pulsing at the center of my forehead.

In a flash of clarity, I caught a fleeting glimpse of the ugly truth, and I had an epiphany: I had become a monster.

———

My memories of the flight to Arizona and the days immediately following my arrival are obscured, perhaps because time has danced on the details for too many years, and perhaps because I was starved literally out of my mind when the events themselves occurred. Recollections come as bitten off frames of film, spliced together over the years as I have tried mentally to edit my memories into something coherent. I remember my mother's car pulling out of our driveway late at night as we headed for Midway airport. I wore heather gray one-piece cotton pajamas from Victoria's Secret (fine lingerie seems such a waste on a skeleton) with a heavy gray Gap logo sweatshirt as a top layer. In the backseat, I tucked my security blanket under my head and gave up my fight against sleep. My grandmother Mimi, in the early stages of Alzheimer's, was along for the trip, partly for companionship for my mother and partly for her own protection and supervision. Every ten minutes, she would comment to Mom: "Pat, I'm worried about our Jena. She's so skinny, don't you think?" My mother, at that time the patron saint of patience, would explain over and over that I was sick and we were, in fact, on our way to fly me out west for treatment. The discussion would repeat itself verbatim, a tape stuck on continuous loop.

We must have checked our bags and boarded the plane, because my next memory is of my mother offering me a bagel with cream cheese as we awaited takeoff. I, of course, refused it. Her response still haunts me: she laughed and said in a vindicated tone, "Fine, but as of tomorrow morning, you'll be eating two thousand calories a day whether you like it or not!"

She could not possibly have known the fear that such a threat (as I saw it) would strike in me. As if to punctuate her words, the plane lurched forward and began its course full speed ahead down the runway while I leaned my head against the window and let a helpless tear slide down my cheek.

Moments later, once we had climbed to a higher altitude, my blood pressure dropped and I braced myself for the familiar sensations: my fingers and toes went numb and tingly, my head loosened itself off my neck and floated away from my body, out the window of the plane into the atmosphere, while my vision gave way to a kaleidoscope of circular spots, flashing black, pink, and green. My mother must have taken my sudden stillness for sleep, for the next thing I knew she was rousing me to look out my window at the aerial view of the Grand Canyon.

"Jen, look here, honey, want some peanuts?"

(No thanks, Mimi.)

"What, you don't want any?"

(No thank you, Mimi.)

"Why not, honey? Look, I have two bags of 'em. Here!"

(Really, Mimi, you eat them. I'm not hungry.)

"But honey, you're too skinny! Boys don't like skinny girls. Here!"

(But I don't want any, Mimi. You eat them, okay?)

"Oh, come on, I have plenty. You should eat more. Pat, she looks thin to me."

(She's sick, Mimi. Remember I told you? She has anorexia.)

"What? Oh, no. Oh, dear . . . Hey, watch my purse while I go to the potty." Mom and I stretched our necks above the heads of passengers, watching to be sure Mimi made it to the bathroom and back to her seat without getting disoriented. As she took her seat, Mom handed Mimi her purse and her bags of peanuts.

"Ooh, peanuts, I love 'em. Jena, look what I have here, honey!" I smiled wearily and took one of the little bags from her outstretched, arthritic hand. Mimi admonished me, "Eat up, now. You look too skinny. Pat, don't you think so?"

I squeezed the bag of peanuts in my fist and fell into an uneasy dream about a plane that crashed into the Grand Canyon, due to a lack of fuel.

Welcome to Wonderland

*W*e touched down in Phoenix, where I rode in a rental car, got carsick, and threw up on the side of the road. Mimi kept having cravings for ice cream, and we would stop at a Baskin Robbins or a Dairy Queen, get her a sundae, wait for her to eat it, and then get back in the car, only for her to say, before we had made our way out of the parking lot, "Boy, I could sure go for some ice cream!"

My memories of this trip revolve around food. I remember telling myself that we would just have to count the raspberry iced tea I drank at a Denny's as a meal, since it surely contained real sugar. I remember the multiple Chinese restaurants where we dined so I could eat plain steamed rice. I remember my plastic baggy full of every flavor of Trident, and how I systematically color-coded them in rows within the bag. I also remember admitting to myself that perhaps I had become a little obsessive about my gum.

Then there was the vegetable chop suey—my final meal before my official admittance into Wonderland. The night before I was admitted to the Ranch, my mom, Mimi, and I ate in yet another Chinese restaurant. I had become manipulative, calling the shots as to where we would and would not eat. My mother gave in to my every whim, in the hopes that I would eat *something* if I could feel somewhat comfortable. I ordered my usual veggie chop suey, with my safe white rice, and I ate only the broccoli with half a cup of rice. Then, realizing it would be the last meal over which I would exercise any real control, I freaked. I excused myself, went into the dirty restaurant restroom, and took a gigantic handful of orange and blue pills. My heart was already beating strangely, and I had a feeling this one last mega dose of Dulcolax and hydrochlorothiazide (a diuretic) just might kill me.

Early the next morning, around five o'clock, my mother found me lying on the ceramic tile of the bathroom in our motel suite. The laxatives had worked a reverse effect, causing the contents of my stomach to lurch up rather than down, and I had vomited and heaved until I passed out. Whispered prayers swirled like colors in my mind as I lay semiconscious, shivering: *I'm sorry, I'm so sorry. I didn't mean it, I'm sorry.* My mother recalls this incident with clarity and horror: "We had to *peel* you off of that bathroom floor. I thought you were a goner."

Pulling myself slowly out of that particular crisis, I made it to the bed in the hotel room, where I lay for the next hour, while Mom drove into town to buy me a pair of jeans. The Remuda brochure stipulated that patients have a pair of jeans for horseback riding, and I had none that still fit. When Mom returned from the Western store in downtown Wickenburg, AZ, she held out a size-zero pair of Jordache riding jeans, which I peered at with my one open eye. Now I had everything I needed to head out the door to the treatment center—except energy and courage. I seemed to be running short on both.

Either because of stupefying fear or the toxic Dulcolax and hydrochlorothiazide overdose, I do not remember exactly what happened next. I remember a storefront office in a strip mall with the Remuda logo on a sign above the door. I cried, begging my mom to go because if she stayed it would be harder to say good-bye, and watched her cry. I signed a thousand and one consent forms. According to my file, there was an intake interview conducted by a woman named Karen D. These intake forms report that Karen D. observed me as "tearful and moderately depressed, with sluggish movements. Frightened but compliant. Very thin."

I have no recollection of loading my stuff into a van to drive from that downtown office to the Remuda Ranch campus down the road.

Arriving, I remember well.

The van turned off the main thoroughfare onto a narrow road and slowed to a crawl, gravel crunching beneath the tires. My pulse quickened as I surveyed what was to become my home for the next several months. It was picturesque: towering palms flanked the long road, cacti in various shapes and sizes stretched proudly toward the white-hot sun, rustic slat fencing bordered the open fields where quarterhorses meandered in tranquil circles. Beyond the corral, past the paddock, we crept toward the main lodge down the dusty road to the right. To the left, an oddly peaceful sight: a tall wooden cross reached high above the desert gardens against a backdrop of blue sky and wispy clouds. I felt the van's engine go still and looked out at a southwestern style adobe structure with a large iron insignia above the gate: "RR."

"Home sweet home," the nameless driver sang out beside me. I turned and pulled my sunglasses down on my nose, eyeing her cynically with one raised brow.

"Okay," she said, "Maybe not. But you'll like it here. It's kind of like camp. Let's be positive, shall we?"

"I am being positive. I am *positive* that I really do *not* want to be here."

With great physical effort, I wheeled my overstuffed duffel bag through the huge double doors of the main lodge. I entered gingerly, head down, eyes averted, not unlike a scared dog.

"Just give me a moment to get you signed in, and then we'll introduce you to your admitting nurse. Are you okay?"

I allowed myself a nervous laugh. "No."

She smiled. "You will be, I promise."

I found an inconspicuous spot to lean against the wall in the foyer, as I begged my heart to be still. It was *freezing* in the building, and I stared at my feet, conscious of my mottled blue skin dotted with goosebumps the size of small hail. I closed my eyes, drifting in and out of the moment, and repeated my timid, tentative mantra: *you're okay, you're okay, you're okay.*

"Doing okay?"

"What? Oh. Um, yeah. I'm just . . . um . . ."

"Jena? Can you look at me? Look at my eyes, honey. Jena? Whoops! Let's get some apple juice over here."

Juice? Why? What's happening? I don't remember sitting down. Who's touching me?

"Jena, can you hear me?"

"Mmm-hmm . . ."

"We're just going to keep your head down until we can get you some juice, hon. Try and stay with us."

A hand on my neck, holding me down. A hand on my back to soothe me. Another hand coming suddenly into view, inserting a straw into my mouth. A few minutes later, the room stopped spinning, and my caretakers allowed me to give vertical living another try.

Time must have passed; memories unravel, chunks of history gone forever. I next recall sitting on a bed in the main lodge near the nurses' station while an MHT (Mental Health Technician) named Teresa sorted through the luggage, spread out on the bed.

"You can keep your pictures, but I'll need to take the glass out of the frames," she explained as she confiscated items deemed to be contraband. "Just a safety precaution."

"I'm not gonna cut myself," I mumbled, feeling insulted.

"That may be, but we don't want to give any other patients the opportunity. I'm sure you understand."

I watched as the pile of forbidden items grew: nail clippers, mouthwash ("anything with alcohol needs to be checked with nursing"), safety pins ("But they're *safety* pins," I reasoned, to which Teresa replied: "Sorry; can't take any chances."), nail polish, magazines ("these can be triggering") razors, aspirin.

"All items of contraband will be kept in a bin with nursing, and you can check them out per request as needed. Any questions?"

"When do I get my orange jumpsuit?" I asked, too exhausted to keep my sarcasm in check.

"You're in luck—no uniform required," Teresa answered. "But you do get a stylish blue hospital gown. There's one in your drawer; you'll wear it for morning weigh-ins."

"Fabulous."

"Okay," she said, hands on her hips, as she glanced around the room. "We're done here. Next stop, Dr. Hall, the psychologist. This one could take an hour or two; do you need a bathroom break first?"

"If you don't mind. I'll just be a second."

"That's fine, but I have to come with you. It's policy."

"What? You've got to be kidding. I can't even use the restroom by myself?"

"Sorry," Teresa said and shrugged regretfully. "It's for your protection. We need to ensure that no one has an opportunity to purge."

"I *don't* purge. I *swear*. Please just let me go. I can't do this with someone *watching*!"

"You'll learn to. Everyone does."

"This was definitely *not* in the brochure," I drawled as I shuffled into the adjoining bathroom. "I mean, can *you* go to the bathroom in front of people?"

Teresa chuckled as she stood outside the open stall (she was kind enough to look away). "Ha! I grew up in a family of seven; I had no choice!"

"I can't believe this," I whined, as I sat awkwardly on the toilet, utterly unproductive. "Could you, like, sing a song or something?"

"How about if I just keep talking?"

"Fine, just don't take any long pauses," I advised.

"Okay, let's see. So you've had your medical eval with Dr. Jensen, and you're going to consult with the psychologist next for another eval. He's super nice; everyone loves him. By the time that's over, it should be time for dinner."

"You say that like it's a good thing," I moaned, still unable to empty my bladder by so much as a drop.

"Don't worry, we go easy on you for your first meal," Teresa said as she caught herself looking directly at me, then quickly looked away. "Just about done?"

I pulled up my shorts. "It's a lost cause. I give up."

"Then let's not keep Dr. Hall waiting," Teresa said. "Better luck next time."

———

Dr. Hall was a pleasant, fortysomething man with graying hair and a bushy mustache, whose gentle tone and kind eyes softened the blow of his intensive questioning. He watched me keenly, never taking his eyes off me as I spoke. I answered his questions guardedly at first, but gradually disclosing more and more as it became obvious that nothing I said shocked him.

"Having any problems with delusions or hallucinations of any kind? Any thoughts of suicide?"

"No and no."

"Have you been involved in any sort of self-mutilation?"

"Do you mean cutting?"

"Cutting, burning, any other sort of self-harm outside of your eating disorder behaviors?"

"Only twice, a long time ago."

"What did you do?"

"I cut myself and burned my hand with a hair straightener."

"Intentionally?"

"Yes."

"Why did you do it?"

"To make it all stop."

"To make what stop?"

"All the angry thoughts."

"Who were you angry at?"

"Myself."

"Did it work? Did cutting and burning yourself make the angry thoughts go away?"

"Not as well as starving."

Patient presents as a nineteen-year-old female whose physical appearance is consistent with that of her stated age. She was dressed in a casual manner consistent with other residents in the Remuda Ranch milieu. However, she was wearing a long sweatshirt. As a result it was difficult to determine exactly how thin she was, and yet she appeared to be quite thin. Her mood appeared to be dysphoric in that she appeared to be moderately depressed.

"How about racing thoughts?"

"Yes."

"When do you find your thoughts racing?"

"When I lie down to sleep."

"And what are the thoughts of?"

"Food, mostly. Calories and numbers and calculations. I can't turn off my inner calculator."

"That must be annoying."

"Very much, yes."

Patient states that she has intrusive obsessional thoughts about food, but does not appear to have any other obsessions. She does appear to have significant food rituals which are compulsive in nature. She will only eat certain foods out of specific dishes, uses only tiny utensils such as baby spoons. She states that she is quite adamant in these rituals. She also states that she has to have her environment in a very neat order. Although this would not necessarily indicate an obsessive compulsive disorder, it would indicate obsessive thinking with ritualistic compulsions which play a role in her eating disorder.

"History of anxiety problems?"

"Yes."

"When did they begin?"

"When I was in sixth grade. My mom and stepdad were divorcing. It was my first year in junior high, and we had to change for gym and take showers, which freaked me out. I felt like I was the only sixth-grader going through puberty, and I couldn't deal with the idea of letting my friends see me naked."

I reported my issues with puberty and gym class, my visit to the middle-school social worker, and my year of home tutoring, visits with a psychiatrist, and medication with Xanax.

"And were you homeschooled for seventh grade also?"

"Nope. Seventh grade was great."

"What was different in seventh grade?"

"All of my friends had curves by then, too."

"Hmm."

Patient expresses a great deal of self-loathing related to body image disturbance. Patient attributes this body dissatisfaction to early-onset puberty.

"Okay, Jena, I'm sending you out of here with homework today," Dr. Hall warned as he produced a thick stack of electronically scored test booklets. "These are psychological profiling tests. I'd like you to work on them today and tomorrow and then turn them in to your case therapist. She'll get them back to me. They're long, and they're pretty invasive and involved; just try to answer as honestly as you can and be sure not to skip any questions."

SUMMARY OF CLINICAL ISSUES:

Severe eating disordered behavior and attitudes

Depression as manifested by: depressed mood, isolation, anhedonia, self-depreciation, hyposomnia alternating with insomnia, indecisiveness, decreased ability to concentrate

Anxiety as manifested by: excessive worry, physiological manifestations of anxiety

Separation individuation issues/enmeshment with mother

Apparent fears of maturation and sexual development

Unresolved issues related to trauma, possible PTSD issues

Over-controlled emotionally

Dependency issues

Severe body image disturbance

Spiritual distress

Suspiciousness

Low self-esteem

PROVISIONAL DIAGNOSES:

AXIS I: *Anorexia Nervosa, Restricting Type*
           Depression, Not Otherwise Specified
           Anxiety Disorder, Not Otherwise Specified
AXIS II: *No Diagnosis*
AXIS III: *Per Medical*
AXIS IV: *Moderate-Severe*
AXIS V: *Global Assessment of Functioning (Scale of*
           0–100): GAF 25

*O*ne of the first residents to capture my attention, and subsequently my heart, was Andrea. About thirty minutes after being admitted, I stood in line at the med window outside the day room, awaiting my first ration of supplements and happy pills. I caught sight of her out of the corner of my eye: long chestnut hair, wavy and wild, translucent skin pale as a ghost's, nasogastric tube in her nose, pushing her IV pole gingerly, looking straight ahead with an intense, icy blue stare. I studied her. She seemed incredibly sad or frightened or both, but she had an almost ethereal glow about her. Had she not been so visibly fragile and ill, one might have mistaken her for an angel.

After I had dutifully swallowed my little cup of capsules, the med nurse asked if I had any questions. "Yes, actually," I answered quietly, leaning forward on the counter. "Who is that girl walking by the window?"

The nurse, Sandy, smiled and nodded as if she had been expecting me to ask. "That's Andrea. She's been here a few months now. Would you like me to introduce you?"

"No," I replied absently, continuing to watch the sad angel. "I'll go and say hi in a minute."

"Okay, but don't take it personally when she doesn't answer," Sandy warned. "Andrea isn't talking yet."

"She isn't talking? Not ever?"

"No, she used to speak. But not since she has been sick, and not at all in the months she has been here," Sandy sighed as she closed my chart. "But who knows? Maybe she'd like someone to give it another shot. Most of the other gals just leave her to herself these days."

I noticed that it was true: no one said a word to Andrea. She may as well have been furniture in that room. She had ended her slow pilgrimage to one of the rustic, log-style couches and lay on her back, in her odd, still way, one hand resting on her belly, the other on her chest. I decided to say hello. After all, I didn't know anyone else.

"Hi," I said awkwardly. I motioned to the chair beside her. "Anyone sitting here?"

Slow, sad shake of her head.

"Mind if I sit?"

She shrugged in slow motion. For a while neither of us spoke. Finally, I tried again: "This is my first day."

Nothing.

"Have you been here long?"

She nodded, looking at my feet.

I wondered what would happen if my questions didn't have yes-or-no answers, and so I asked her name. Her eyes moved from my feet to my knees, and she managed to say "Andrea" in a voice somehow *smaller* than a whisper.

"Well, it's nice to meet you. I guess you're my first friend here . . . Lucky you!"

It was the most beautiful thing I had seen in weeks: Andrea's still, blue lips formed a very slight, slow smile, nearly redeeming my day from the pit of despair. In true anorexic fashion, I had already managed to divert my attention to someone else's issues instead of my own. I had a friend, but beyond that, I had a project.

_____

Late afternoon, following my initial intake interviews and exams, I sat, curled into a tiny ball of fear and resistance, in a corner of the day room, knees pulled tight to my chest, my sweatshirt stretched over them. I must have resembled a bright red cocoon with a pained, grimacing face. I had been attempting to scrawl frantic, panicked thoughts into my journal, but I mostly just held my pen in a Kung Fu grip and sat, taking in the sights and sounds. It seemed a thousand voices filled the room, streaming in bitten-off sentences that floated past my ears:

"Cora, I'll need the phone after you. How much longer?"

"Man, I miss my boyfriend . . ."

"I am, like, *so* ticked off at my therapist right now . . ."

"I told her I was *raised* a vegan. That is so *not* a disorder . . ."

"My husband flies in on Friday . . ."

"Why does it have to be soooo cold in here?"

"I totally lost it in group today . . ."

"My insurance is pulling out after the fifth . . ."

Turning my ear toward the nurses' station behind the med window, I overheard conversations of a different sort:

"Is he increasing her Klonopin?"

"Andrea gets the Resource through her tube now. She won't drink it."

"File this one under New Residents. She admitted at four o'clock . . ."

"Kristy hides the Neurontin under her tongue; she did it again this morning . . ."

"Make sure Natalie gets the regular Colace with dinner . . ."

"Did you take my pen? I'm gonna chain this pen to the counter from now on!"

"Something smells good in there . . ."

The last comment turned my stomach. My first meal as an inpatient was just minutes away, and the fear was paramount. I had been told by my admitting nurse that the first meal was considered a "grace meal," meaning we were not required to finish it, or to eat it at all, for that matter. I suppose it was Staff's merciful way of empowering us to choose how we began our treatment. Would we dive in headlong, surrendering to the program with determination to conquer our demons, or linger just one more night safely on the shore, refusing to even get our feet wet? I chose the latter. I would be willing to wager that nearly all the residents refuse that first meal, whether they secretly wanted it or not, because it was a statement that seemed crucial for us to make: I will eat, but only under duress, because I do not *want* to eat.

Baloney. The truth is, there is nothing any of us wanted more desperately. When you are starving, part of you will gravitate toward food as a plant grows toward sunlight. You will dream about it—inane, frightening dreams about tossing the contents of someone else's refrigerator into a blender and slurping it up through a straw. You will dream you are in a bizarre video game, in which ice cream cones are falling from the sky like hail, and if you are unable to dodge them, you gain weight and the game is over. You will dream a vivid dream about eating a Belgian waffle with thousands of eyes watching you, although you've never had a Belgian waffle in your life. As strange and surreal as these crazy dreams are, you will awaken from them in a cold sweat and remind yourself quickly that it was just another food dream, and you had not actually eaten anything that you dreamt about. To prove it to yourself, you will press hard on your concave belly, pushing deeper until you feel that ever-comforting lump: your spine.

As I awaited that first dinner, I knew those late-night body checks were over. I was going to be made to eat; there was no way around it. Eventually, I would gain weight. No matter how hard I fought it, it was *going to happen*. The thrill of lying alone in a dark room and feeling my bones would soon be gone, replaced by an unimaginable panic at the metamorphosis of a body I would no longer wish to claim as my own. Imagine being told that over the next few months, you are systematically going to mutate beyond recognition into the thing you fear most, and you will begin to understand the horrific anxiety an eating disordered person feels as she stands at the brink of unwelcome physical restoration.

"Med window is open," a friendly voice sang out over the commotion of clinking cookware and gabbing girls, and a flock of patients migrated toward her for their mealtime round of multicolored pills in tiny paper cups.

Still not quite knowing the drill, I finally filed into line behind a girl I had not seen before. She had waist-length, fine blond hair, curled into loose ringlets at the ends. A good head shorter than myself, she stood with her feet spread apart and turned outward, like a duck. She wore an old pair of faded Levi's (which might have fit her at one time, but now hung from her like a sack, which is what jeans do when there is no rear end inside them) and a blue, plaid flannel shirt. She probably registered that I was the only one in line not engaged in a conversation.

"Hey," she said.

"Hey," I said.

She said, "You new?"

I said, "Yep. You?"

She smiled, fidgeting with nervous energy. "What gave me away? The fact that I'm about to curl into a fetal position on the floor from the smell of whatever they're daring to call dinner?"

I laughed, truly relieved to find someone who thought the way I did. "You, too? Well, make room for me down there. I just may join you."

She laughed uneasily and pulled her long hair into a ponytail, holding an elastic band in her teeth as she said, "I'm Tiffany." She took the band out of her teeth to wrap around her hair and added, "But there's another Tiffany here, which has already caused some confusion, so just call me Tiff."

"Got it," I said. "I'm Jena."

"So is this your grace meal, or whatever it's called?"

"Yeah. I admitted after lunch, so I haven't had the pleasure of a mandatory meal yet. Tomorrow morning is when the real fun begins."

"Ugh, for me, too," Tiff said, wincing. "Maybe they'll seat us next to each other so we can hold hands or something to get through it."

"Right," I laughed. "Something tells me they don't serve celery and Diet Coke for breakfast."

"And sugar-free Jell-O."

"Hey, we must have been on the same meal plan!" I joked.

"Seriously!" Tiff laughed. "The peel-me-off-the-floor plan. When you pass out from malnutrition, you know you're doing *really* well."

"Exactly!" I said, playing along. "And if you're really successful, you win a trip to Arizona."

"But there's a catch: you have to stay in the most freezing cold air-conditioned resort in the entire desert."

"I know!" I said. "I would give anything just to step outside for five minutes to defrost."

"Oh, didn't you get that speech yet?"

"No, what speech?"

"Apparently, the desert heat could kill us because we are already dehydrated. It's a wonder we didn't drop dead walking from the van into the building this afternoon." It was becoming clear that Tiff would be a good source of sarcasm, if ever I should need it. As it turned out, I would need it regularly, and Tiff and I would become fast friends.

"So we can't *ever* go outside?" I asked.

"Only once in the early morning and once after 4:00 in the afternoon, and only for ten minutes—in the shade."

"Are you kidding?" I asked again, glad I had packed sweatshirts.

"Nope. Those are the rules, until we're 'medically stable.'"

"Well, there's nothing 'medically stable' about hypothermia," I drawled facetiously.

"Tiffany Sanders?" The med nurse asked as Tiff approached the window with no small air of caution. "Welcome to Remuda. I'm Sandy. Let's see what all we have for you here . . ."

Tiff raised her eyebrows and glanced at me. "What *all*? I should only have Paxil."

"Well, you'll have a chance to get that squared away with the psychiatrist when you meet with him in the morning. For now, it looks like all we have for you is the Paxil, a multivitamin, Metamucil, and the Colace."

"What's Colace?"

"A laxative, dear."

"Oh, thank *God*," Tiff said and downed the cup of pills in one quick gulp.

"Open your mouth, please," Sandy said, taking the empty cup. "I need to be sure they all made it down."

"Seriously? You have to do a *mouth check*?"

Sandy shrugged. "Everybody gets it, not just the new girls."

Tiff rolled her eyes and opened her mouth, sticking her tongue out at the nurse. Having passed the test, she tossed her ponytail over her shoulder and turned to me. "All yours."

I swallowed my cup of pills, showed Sandy my empty mouth, and took my cup of Metamucil with me as Tiff and I made our way toward the dining hall. I frowned into my cup, stirring the grainy mixture and watching in disgust as it began to congeal. "Ah, nothing like a good fiber cocktail to kick off happy hour."

Tiff clicked her plastic cup against mine. "Here's to your regularity."

"And to yours," I laughed. "Cheers!"

Just before bedtime, I made another friend, with whom I would become especially close. She was in line at the med window, her extremely bony arms wrapped around her as she curled into herself as if imploding. A curious-looking creature, quite tall, who appeared to weigh about as much as half a feather, this was Nina. I found myself marveling at the way the back of her ankle was nothing more than a naked cord wrapped in paper-thin skin, the way her body didn't seem to be there at all, the way her face seemed to express a silent apology. I wanted to introduce myself. I needed an ice-breaker. We were both freezing, and that was common ground.

"Could it be any colder in here?" I asked, taking my place in line behind Nina.

"Hmm?" Nina asked, a forced, too-sweet smile wrinkling her sunken, hollow, strangely beautiful face.

"It's cold," I repeated, shivering as though we were playing charades.

"Oh, I know," she said, the forced smile still frozen in place.

"I'm Jena," I said, half-extending my hand, still tucked inside the extra-long sleeve of my sweatshirt.

"Nina," she said, taking my sleeve. Even the way she spoke her name sounded like an apology.

I wish I could remember that first conversation, which must have been poignant and meaningful and tender, because soon

Nina became my best friend in treatment. At that point, I may simply have been attracted to the idea of befriending the sickest-looking person in the room and God used my sick motives to grow a beautiful friendship that has endured to this day.

Whatever we talked about, the encounter left an impression, because my mother has a letter from me, scrawled on Mickey Mouse stationery, in which I gushed about meeting Nina. "I think we will end up being friends. Maybe she can be like a mother to me here; she's probably in her fifties."

When I found this letter a year ago, I cringed. I considered calling Nina to apologize. When Nina and I met, she was thirty-two.

Off to a Rough Start

*M*y first night in treatment I had to sleep in the main lodge, near the nurses' station, on close medical monitoring. Despite the glare of lights and frequent room checks, I fell quickly into a heavy sleep until, suddenly, out of the deep blue somewhere of my slumber, I vomited violently all over myself. They had given me Perdiem, a fiber laxative, at the night med window. Evidently, my compromised and abused digestive system could not handle the fiber and defiantly tossed it back.

In an instant, a sweet MHT named Sharon was at my bedside, gushing over me with her Texan drawl. "Oh, honey, what's happened here? Oh, you poor dear. Goodness, the first night is always rough, but I'd say you're havin' it a little rougher than most! Here, sweetie." She grabbed a Kleenex from the bedside table and wet it with my water bottle, wiping at my cheeks and forehead as she cooed maternally, "There, there. I may not be your mama, but you'll find I'm the next best thing while you're here. Let's get you washed up, darlin'." She took a closer look at the damage and called for backup, summoning an efficient team of nurses and techs to get me clean and changed, check my vitals, express their compassion.

Twenty minutes later, exhausted and sore from retching, I was asleep again, but thirty minutes later, I was jolted awake in a repeat performance. In came the cleanup squad once more—and twice again before night gave way to dawn. I apologized profusely between gags and heaves for causing them all so much trouble, for keeping the other residents awake, for making a mess, for being there at all.

Mercifully, morning came, and there had been a changing of the guard. Sharon came in once more just before seven o'clock to check on me and say good-bye before going home. We made small talk about how tired she was, how she had become used to crawling into bed just after the sun came up, how I would have a long day ahead of me—my first day "in the program."

The program began with a daily weigh-in, in a little pine-paneled room off the dining hall, adorned with an examination table, a towering, threatening medical scale, blood pressure cuffs, tiny square mirror mounted five feet above the floor. Over the next several months, I would find this strategic lack of a single full-length mirror anywhere on the grounds endlessly frustrating. All the residents were assigned designated weigh-in times at five-minute intervals, at which we were to arrive in the exam room dressed only in our blue paper hospital gowns, freezing under the relentless draft of the air conditioners.

When it was your turn, you shuffled in half-asleep, mumbled good morning to the cheerful tech, climbed upon the miniature stage backward, facing *away* from the numbers—which was a strict rule, never up for debate—and listened, suddenly wide-awake and trembling with fear, as the tech slid the metal weights across the balance bar, which always seemed to take *forever.*

The next few days crowd themselves together in my memory, a magazine-cutout collage of mental images: women introducing themselves, women crying and laughing and screaming and apologizing, staff members making formal introductions and preparing me for what was to come, Tiff and me sitting beside one another at a table in the dayroom, groaning to one another as we completed a seemingly endless series of psychological assessment tests. "If I wasn't suicidal when I started these stupid things, I will be by the time I finish," Tiff moaned.

Tiff and I were nearing the end of our stack of tests when I heard a voice call my name over the din in the crowded day room, where young women gathered in groups, laughing and playing Yahtzee and coloring in coloring books like seven-year-olds.

"Yeah?"

"I need you to come with me for a minute, sweetie." This kind young woman, a physician's assistant wearing purple scrubs and a sweet smile, was holding my chart propped against her chest.

I glanced at Tiff and winced. "This can't be good."

Tiff pulled a cynical face, as only she could: "It never is."

I hopped off my pillow on the floor a little too quickly, blacked out for a second or two (*when will I learn?*), and stepped over the bodies of my fellow residents splayed on the floor beneath their layers of sweatpants and fluffy socks.

"Am I in trouble?" I asked, joking.

"We don't know yet," she said, clearly *not* joking.

I followed her, the sharp *squeak-squeak* of her impossibly white shoes scraping my brain. She led me into the examination room, and my heart rate quickened instinctively. She gestured to a knotty-pine chair next to the desk and invited me to sit. She opened my chart on the desk and clasped her hands between her knees as she faced me squarely, eye-to-eye.

"Okay," she said. "Here's the deal: we just got your blood work back from the lab, and you are one out-of-whack little kiddo."

I decided I liked her. "I could have told you that."

"Well, your levels are all over the place. Your potassium is dangerously low, and although that is definitely not a good thing, we expected that. What we didn't expect to find . . ." She eyed me suspiciously, as if expecting me to finish her sentence. I didn't.

"Yeah? What?" I shifted in the hard chair and tucked a flat palm behind my aching spine.

"What we did not expect to find was a completely whacked-out TSH reading. Do you know what that means?"

I lowered my eyebrows and shook my head.

"TSH is Thyroid Stimulating Hormone, and yours is extremely low."

She stared at me for what seemed like an eternity. I leaned in a bit closer: "Um, are you waiting for me to say something?"

"Well," she said, pulling the open file onto her lap, "I thought you might like to tell me what you know about this."

"Nothing," I said defensively. "I didn't even know what a TSH was until just now."

"Right. And now that you know what it is, would you like to tell me what you have been doing to manipulate yours?"

I stared a hole into her shoe. She might have even felt it, because she moved her sneakered foot to nudge my sandaled one gently. She cocked her head and fixed me with that eye-to-eye gaze again: "What are you taking, Jena?"

"Nothing, anymore."

"What were you taking, until three days ago?"

"Just the usual."

"The usual purgatives, you mean? Laxatives and diuretics?"

"And uppers."

"Uppers?"

"Vivarin, No-Doz, you know—stimulants."

"Jena, caffeine pills don't do this sort of thing to a person's thyroid." Her conspiratorial tone began to break me down. She knew something. She was on to me. "So you were taking purgatives, stimulants—and what else, Jena?"

My face went hot, and I stared at the part of the floor where her squeaky white shoe had been, and mumbled shamefully, "Thyroid."

"Mmm-hmm," she nodded. "And where did you get it? Was your physician back home aware that you were taking thyroid?"

"No. She didn't prescribe it."

"Who did?"

My response was barely audible: "Our vet."

She leaned back and made a face that I couldn't help but smile at. "Vet . . . erin*arian*??"

I nodded, suddenly fighting back a giggle.

"The *vet* wrote you a script for Synthroid?"

"Not quite. My *dog's* vet wrote a script for generic thyroxine . . . for the *dog*."

"Uh-huh . . ." She was looking at me sideways now, and I decided I definitely liked her. She was funny. "So if you were taking doggie thyroid, how many were you taking, my child?"

"Five . . . at a time."

"How many times a day?"

"Twice."

"So *ten* a day?"

I nodded.

She suddenly looked horrified, and for the first time in a few minutes, I felt a little scared. "For how long?"

"Five or six months, I guess."

She took off her funky tortoise-shell glasses, lowered her head, and rubbed the bridge of her nose, wincing. The humor had gone completely. She asked if I had the pills with me, as if she dreaded the answer. I said I hadn't brought any pills with me, which was the truth. When she finally looked up, her eyes were red, her skin blotchy. She put her glasses on again and said quite decidedly, "We'll have to do a room search anyway."

"Fine," I said. "Whatever. You won't find anything."

"I believe you," she said, which meant a lot to me. Then she added, "But you just lost your level, I'm afraid."

"Level 1A again?"

"Uh, yep."

"24-hour watch?"

"Uh, yep."

"Medically unstable?"

Her sense of humor returned. "See how much you're learning?"

That afternoon, after my room search turned up zilch, I met with Jody, the nutritionist. She gave me an informative booklet on the American Dietetic Association's Food Exchange System. Many treatment facilities use this program, which plays down triggering approaches like calorie counting and instead focuses on portions and variety of food required by each individual. Rather than assigning a patient a goal of 600 calories per meal, for example, the exchange system might require that the patient receive 2 lean meat exchanges, 2 carbohydrate exchanges, 1 fruit, 1 vegetable, 1 fat, and so on. Looking at my assigned exchange plan now, I see it was truly not excessive in any way. I was initially started on just 800 calories a day, to give my system a chance to transition back into digesting food, but at the time, it seemed as though the amount of food I was expected to consume would kill me.

"I'm sorry," I said to Jody, closing the booklet. "I don't think I can do this."

Jody smiled, smoothing her dark hair off her forehead. "Yes, you can."

"No," I said. "You don't understand. You're asking me to eat as much food in one day as I have been eating in almost a week. I can't do this."

"You've been doing it for two days," Jody said, placating me, "and it hasn't killed you. Your body will adjust; you just have to be patient with it."

"All of the food is *right here*," I said, gripping my distended belly, fighting back tears. "I feel like I am eating constantly. Normal people do not eat like this."

Jody smiled. "Jena, I think you'll agree you have lost sight of what normal *is*. Right now, you have to trust me. I know what I am talking about, and I would not overfeed you. I also would not underfeed you. These are the exchanges your body requires. You have to trust me."

She's making you fat, the voice whispered. *You've got to get out of here.*

"It's too much food," I insisted. "I can't."

"Okay," Jody said. "Well, this brings us to the other thing I need to discuss with you." She moved the exchange booklet to the floor and addressed me softly. "I suggested a feeding tube when I met with your team last night, and they agreed it would help get you through this rough patch at the beginning. You wouldn't feel so overwhelmed by the food."

"A tube?" I responded, stunned. "No."

"It won't give you more nutrition; you will be given the same amount you are being given now—at least for a little while—but you won't actually have to eat quite as much until you start to feel more comfortable."

I stared at my hands, shaking my head.

Jody continued, "I think it's a good idea."

"No," I repeated.

"Will you think about it? Take the day to think it over, and let me know."

"What did my case therapist say?" I asked.

"Deb thinks it would be helpful."

"What about everyone else?" I probed. Surely *someone* on my "treatment team" must have felt this was a drastic move. I waited.

"Everyone agrees," Jody said. "Nursing agrees, your physician agrees, and the MHTs who have observed you for meals these past two days think it would relieve a lot of your anxiety at mealtimes. This is not meant to be a punishment, Jena. We just want to help you."

"Hmm," I said, cynically.

"You do not *have* to consent," Jody added. "You're an adult."

"But everyone thinks I should," I said, feeling trapped.

"It's not that we feel you *should*. The team believes it would be beneficial."

I sighed. I looked around the busy dayroom, counting. Six girls had feeding tubes. None looked miserable, at least not at that particular moment. One, a girl my age named Ginger, was laughing with a friend by the telephones. My head was full: Should I do it? *It will only make you FAT that much quicker.* Will the team be disappointed in me if I don't consent? Is it important to please them? Can they keep me longer if I don't? *They don't care about you; they just want more money out of you. Don't be stupid!* Will it really only give me the same number of calories I'm getting now? *If you get that tube, you will have ZERO control. Do you really want to let other people decide what goes into your body? They could load you up while you're sleeping. You're such a fat idiot. Don't even THINK about it.*

"Well, think about it," Jody chimed in, as if on cue. "Think it over, talk it over with Deb, pray about it. You can let me know later." Jody left me to ponder, panic, and pray.

This was a problem. As I had discovered in therapy with Meg, my need to please other people and keep everyone happy had never served me well. I cared too much what others thought of my decisions; I labored under the assumption that displeasing others equaled rejection from them. I also labored under a palpable fear of losing control, which is precisely what the implantation of a feeding tube signaled to me.

I was a mess the rest of the day. I talked it over with Deb, my new case therapist, who clearly supported the idea of "The Tube." I talked it over with Tiff, who thought it would help me not to stress out at the table, since it would mean less food on my plate. I even called my high school voice teacher back in Illinois. I asked her if having a tube running along my throat could damage my vocal chords, hoping she would forbid me to do it, thus letting me off the hook. She told me the best thing I could do for my voice would be to get healthy. No one was telling me what I wanted to hear.

"What are your reasonable concerns about the feeding tube?" Deb asked during our session the next morning.

"That it will just make me fat more quickly than eating would," I said honestly.

"That's a concern, but not a reasonable one," Deb countered. "What reasonable concerns do you have?"

"That I won't have control over what goes into my own body."

"Do you have that control now?" Deb asked.

"Not since I've been here," I said sadly. "I have no control over anything."

"Sure you do," Deb said, her small brown eyes squinting at me. "You could leave."

"Which would disappoint people and make everybody mad at me."

"Maybe."

"So I have no control."

"Not over others' reactions and emotions, no," Deb said,

seemingly pleased with her quick comeback. "So what's the real concern?"

"Either way, I disappoint someone or tick somebody off."

"Who do you tick off if you refuse the feeding tube?"

"Everyone here."

"People who want you to be healthy and enjoy your life?" Deb asked.

"Supposedly."

"Okay," she said, "and who do you tick off if you consent to the feeding tube?"

"Myself."

"But you'll be angry with yourself either way, won't you? Either for giving up control—as you see it—or for letting people down. Either way, you can't please yourself. You're a tough critic, Jena."

"Yes."

"So if the people who care about you want you to be well, who else is there to tick off? Who would possibly be upset with you for taking a step to help yourself get well?"

I played dumb.

"Let me put it this way," Deb said. "If Jesus came to give you life and life more abundantly, and the enemy of your soul roams about like a lion, seeking whom he may destroy, who will be ticked off that you are moving toward restoring your health and enjoying an abundant life?"

I rolled my eyes. "Satan. So if I refuse the tube I'm siding with the Devil?" I asked, exasperated.

"No," Deb said. "But it would be a powerful statement if you didn't refuse it. It would say you are committing yourself to getting healthy, and you are, in fact, relinquishing some control—not to us, but to God. Even if you don't trust your treatment team, Jena, God can be trusted with you and with everything that concerns you."

I sat, silent and still, but with wheels turning inwardly at the speed of light. Finally, I said, "It *has* to be out *before* Family Week."

Deb nodded. "Deal."

———

"All right, I won't say this is going to be pleasant, but I'll try to work quickly."

I sat stiffly on an examination table in a cubbyhole-sized room in an outpatient clinic as the doctor, a round woman with kind eyes and orange kitty cat scrubs, began to prep my nose and throat. She sprayed a local anesthetic into my throat and swabbed something into my right nostril, and it felt as though she were trying to locate my brain via my nose with her endless Q-tip. Involuntarily, I yelped. The voice in my head hissed: *Crybaby.*

Adding to my embarrassment, I felt unwelcome tears come as I watched her assistant wheel a metal cart beside the bed, its contents mocking me, gleaming: surgical tape, pairs of sterilized scissors, gauze, a styrofoam cup of water with a straw, a rolled up length of thin, flexible tubing.

I remember the rest in the third person, as though I watched the procedure from the doorway. There are voices, female, saying, "Swallow, swallow." The patient gags and cries and wants to bolt off the table down the hall, out the seventh-story window. I remember thinking it would be funny to have a photo of this scene made into a postcard to send to friends back home: "Wish you were here!"

During the van ride back to Remuda, I leaned my head against the window, rolling the loose end of my NG tube, tucked behind my right ear, between my finger and thumb. I stared at people in the passing cars as one might watch exotic animals at the zoo, studying their foreign habits. These curious creatures sped past in SUVs and coupes, laughing, talking into cell phones, eating, drinking, smoking, singing along to car stereos, scolding bickering children. Some tried to read while driving, some steered with one hand and rummaged around on passenger seats for nameless things they had lost. Some were thin; some were fat. Some were professionally dressed; some wore shorts and T-shirts. *Not one* other person on the freeway had a tube in his nose.

Digging In

*M*y first two weeks of one-on-one sessions with Deb were awkward and frustrating, in part because I had not yet gained enough weight to improve my cognitive functioning, which is most helpful to the therapeutic process. Most days I sat in her tiny office, wrapped like a papoose in the sleeves of my oversized sweatshirt, and struggled to identify my complicated feelings, let alone describe them in a manner even somewhat coherent.

"What are you aware of, Jena?" Deb asked one day near the end of a particularly fruitless session. She had been eyeing me intently and seemed slightly bemused with my silence, which annoyed me. "What are you thinking when your face scrunches up like that?"

"I wasn't 'aware' my face was scrunched up. Sorry."

"Are you experiencing feelings of guilt right now, Jena?"

"I don't know. Probably."

"Do you experience guilt feelings much of the time?"

"You could say that," I said, shifting uncomfortably.

"Where does the guilt come from?"

"Don't know," I mumbled, deciding to shut down my

responses for a while. I found it all tiring, and I was frustrated with myself for not knowing how to answer Deb's strategic questioning.

"What do you get from feeling guilty, Jena?" Deb asked, prying further. "What does your guilt accomplish?"

I shrugged.

"Does guilt motivate you to change? Or does it paralyze you and keep you stuck in your circumstances?"

Another shrug was all I would volunteer. Deb jotted notes in her mysterious blue notebook, the contents of which I would gladly have paid to see.

Deb tucked her pen behind her ear and cocked her shaggy brown head. "What are you aware of, Jena?"

"I don't even *understand* that question. What are *you* aware of?" I asked sarcastically.

"Well," Deb began, "I am aware of a very angry young woman, and I am wondering what the anger is about and where it is coming from."

"I'm not angry."

"I disagree. I believe you are quite angry, Jena."

"That's your perception."

"But even if a perception is incorrect, it is still valid," Deb responded. "Perception is subjective, not objective. My perception is that you are a very angry girl, who may not realize she is angry. How do you respond to my perception?"

"With indifference."

Deb smiled, entertained by my understated hostility. "Does it bother you to be seen as angry?"

"I'm not angry," I insisted. "I just want to go home."

"I understand that, but does it bother you to be perceived as angry?"

"When I'm not angry it does," I replied, refusing to meet her eyes. The truth, I recognized, was that I was angry with myself for feeling so annoyed with this woman who was attempting to help me. The more I told myself I had no right to be annoyed with her, the more she annoyed me. It was a double bind.

"Does it make you angry that I think you are angry?" Deb asked, allowing herself a wry smile at the irony.

"Yes, all right? Are you happy?"

Deb whispered, "I feel relieved for you, Jena. You've allowed yourself to admit a very organic feeling."

"I'm so happy our session has left *you* feeling better. Can I go now?"

⸻

Two weeks into my stay, something in me snapped. It must have finally hit home that I no longer had any control over my body and eating habits. Short of leaving against medical advice, there was nothing I could do to stop the steady flow of nutrients passing into my body or to escape the relentless progression of meals I was expected to consume without dispute.

I had a five-minute recess in the morning when I was allowed to sit outside. I had been using the time to soak up as much Arizona sun as I could, to return some warmth to my perpetually chilled body. On this particular morning, my thoughts raced as I sneaked off to a quiet spot beneath a shady tree. I felt a compelling need to release my frustration and regain some of the control I had relinquished, and I needed a secluded place to figure out how to do this.

I considered pulling out my feeding tube and wondered if it would even be possible. I held my breath a moment, reached up, and ventured a quick tug. I instantly gagged, tears stinging my eyes and running down my cheek under my sunglasses. Resolutely, I regained my composure and tried again: same result. I wished for a safety pin to poke tiny holes in the tube, so I could perforate it enough to snap it in two. Safety pins, though, were contraband.

Growing desperate to act out in some way, some way violent toward my body and myself, I searched the ground for a rock sharp enough to do damage. My emotions seemed to click off. As if on autopilot, I picked up a rough-edged desert stone and rubbed it against the back of my left hand, hard as I could, back and forth, back and forth, until my hand was raw.

The physical pain was enormous, but there would be no tears. My brain had learned not to respond, and so it refused to release the signal to cry, only to recognize in some cerebral way that the pain had, in fact, moved from inside to outside. Once I made that realization, I placed my bleeding left hand in the pocket of my sweatshirt and went indoors, sat down for yet another meal, and smiled.

"Today we're going to try an exercise in free-association, or stream-of-consciousness, journaling," Deb announced in process group on one gray afternoon. She handed out notebook paper to us as she stepped through the pile of bodies slumped on her office floor. "I want you just to write, write, write—anything that comes to mind, any thoughts and ideas, just write them as they occur to you. Your pen should keep moving, pretty much nonstop. I don't want you to edit yourself in any way. Whatever you think, you write."

It seemed too good to be true: finally, a medium in which I could express myself. No more pesky *talking*. Eagerly, I poised my pen above the paper and awaited Deb's magic words: "You may begin."

So this is free-association. Hmm. Kind of cool. Like that word game we used to play in the car on long trips where one

*person says a word and the next person says a word that it
made them think of, and so on. Let's see . . . Deb. Therapy.
Counselor. Career. College. Quitter. Failure. Fat.*

Well, that was quick.

*Why am I so sarcastic? Ally has a T-shirt that says,
"Sarcasm is the mind's natural defense against stupid." I love
it. I should write sayings for T-shirts. I should write greetings
cards. I should write children's books. I should write letters
to everyone back home. I should write. I should write for a
living!*

*I don't know how to write. I'm just kidding myself. I'm
having delusions of grandeur. I'm having a rapid cycle mixed
bipolar episode.*

And obviously I need to stop reading the Diagnostic and
Statistical Manual of Mental Disorders *for kicks. Only
crazy people read up on crazy. Maybe I am bipolar after all.
I'm the queen of the world! I'm the scum of the earth. Stop—
you're both right!*

*I'm not the scum of the earth. I am salt and light. I am
a reflection of my Creator. I was created for His glory. I am
fearfully and wonderfully made. I am God's workmanship.
I am a new creation. I am being transformed daily by the
renewing of my mind.*

*I need a new mind. I need a new body. I need a new
groove. I need a new hairstyle. I need new clothes. I need a
new pen!*

*I'm using a new pen. See how easy that was? I allowed
myself to admit a need, and I got my need met, and so now
I have a new pen. What a beautiful thing. It's just pure
serendipity. What a funny word. This pen writes purple. Purple
is a funny word. Purple rhymes with nothing. I rhyme with
nothing. Oh Deb, I feel purple today.*

Hey, we didn't do a feelings check-in today! Great, now

how am I supposed to know what I am feeling? If a tree falls in the forest and there is no one there to hear it, does it still make a sound? If we don't open group with a feelings check-in, am I still feeling my feelings?

They've gotten to me. I'm talking psychobabble. I'm drunk on their Kool-Aid.

There I go with the sarcasm again. Is sarcasm really so bad? It probably is. Hey, was this supposed to be a prayer? Did I misunderstand the assignment? God, I would feel awful if I was supposed to be talking to You this whole time, and I've just been scribbling on and on about drinking Kool-Aid and feeling purple.

Thank You for your patience with me. Teach me patience. Teach me mercy. Teach me kindness. Teach me love. Melt me, mold me, use me, fill me. Humor me. HELP ME.

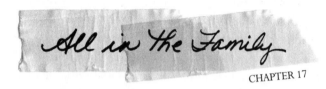

All in the Family

amily Week sneaked up on me, and I felt completely unprepared to see my parents and my sister. At first my father, who had moved to Nevada just a few months before, was reluctant to come because he had started a big job doing electrical work for a new casino. Ultimately, though, he consented, which presented a new reason for my anxiety to flare up: my parents would be in the same room for the first time since I was a child. Also, although I was still a ways off from meeting my weight restoration goal, I felt horribly ashamed at the thought of my family seeing me heavier.

"You look so much better!" Mom gushed when she and my sister, Erica, arrived at the Ranch. She quickly added, "And yes, you're still skinny" as though my thoughts were scrolling across my forehead for all to read.

The three of us sat at a table on the back patio of the main lodge, catching up on what had transpired in our lives over the past five weeks. My sister was preparing for her fairytale wedding, just three months away, and had brought a folder full of photos, drawings, and magazine clippings of her dress, the bridemaids' dresses, the cake, the flowers, the food. I smiled and nodded and struggled to identify with where she was in her life, which seemed in stark contrast to where I was in mine. Erica was building a future, and I was unsure whether I wanted one at all.

Erica's excitement about her wedding plans helped take up some airtime between the three of us, so I didn't have to think of much to say. I had very little *to* say. I was in a hospital. I went to therapy and group and classes, and I ate six times a day. I hadn't been off the premises in over a month. What was there to share?

Dad arrived the next day, while Mom and Erica were out sightseeing. It had been agreed that Dad would stay for just the first two and a half days of Family Week, so he could get back to work. I showed him around the campus, sat awkwardly with him in the dayroom, not knowing what to say. Being visited in treatment was not pleasant, like being visited at college. It was more akin to being visited in jail. There was a sense that you had been "locked up" for your rebellion, that you should have known better. I wanted my dad to be proud of me; at age nineteen, I felt he should have been visiting me at college, should have had the experience of welling with pride as I talked about my classes, my grades, my promising future. He should have been able to take my picture out of his wallet and show it off to his buddies, saying, "And this is my youngest. She's on the dean's list again this year." Instead, I imagined, he might not have wanted to bring me up to his buddies at all. There's little to brag about when your kid is in rehab.

I barely remember the actual Family Week sessions. I know my three family members had to meet with the family therapist several times before I was introduced into the mix. By the time I entered the room, the tension was palpable. It felt like stepping into a war zone.

Years later, with the benefit of my file full of progress notes, I learned what went down. The family therapist's notes read:

This family clearly has a pattern of mistrusting others in the family, of claiming the other person is either lying, telling half-truths, or that they don't remember things happening the way the person has stated them. There are accusations and allegations of infidelity toward the mother.

The father is the "bad guy" in this family, with both the mother and the sister recounting tales of anger and violence. The father denies allegations of physical violence, but did recognize that he may not remember things the patient remembers. This especially applies to his anger and rage, as he realistically may not remember some things that happened.

The sister and the father have a distant and conflicted relationship. The mother has been married four times. Mother and sister, by their own admission, have "violent tempers" like that of the father. This is an angry and volatile family.

The patient, conversely, does not know how to express her anger. Possibly the fact that she can't express anger outwardly leads her to turn the anger inward and she takes it out on herself with self-punishment. She also tries to be perfect so everyone will be pleased with her and no one will be upset. Patient recognizes the possibility that she may use the eating disorder as a way of being sick in order to give the parents, as well as the father and sister, who are estranged, another focus rather than their relationship conflicts.

Patient has a hard time setting boundaries and asking for what she needs from her parents. Mother was raised to "always do what she was told" and in many ways has lived her life this way, particularly in relationships with abusive men. Patient recognizes that her role of protector for the mother was established in early childhood.

This patient bears the symptoms of the family's dysfunction, wants nothing more than for everyone to live at peace with one another. At one point in the session, when each family *member took turns expressing their love for the patient, the patient essentially erupted at them, shouting, "If you love me, stop fighting with each other!" The patient was able, in this environment, to set boundaries with family members and assert herself, saying that she will no longer be put in the middle of their disagreements.*

By the end of the father's stay, the patient had had a moment to tell him that she loves him and forgives him for his violence in her early years. Relationship between father and patient seems to be in a healthy place of new beginnings. Relationship with patient and mother will require greater effort, to begin healthy separation and break down patterns of enmeshment. Sister and father remain distant; mother and father remain hostile toward each other. Patient recognizes that she can love all three members of her family and does not have to be placed in the middle anymore.

Two vivid memories from Family Week involve my father. I recall the moment I told my father I forgave him. He maintained that he did not remember ever being physically violent, but he admitted it could have happened. And when he admitted this, I saw a single tear fall down his cheek. It was a poignant moment, a quiet gesture that spoke volumes. To me, in that moment, Dad was the strongest, most beautiful man in my world.

The other moment my memory has preserved was my dad agreeing to come back the next morning to join me for chapel. We sat outside, under a big shade tree behind the main lodge, in a huge circle. Dad sat between my sister and me, with Mom on the other side of me. The time came when we would go around the circle and pray aloud. I leaned over and whispered to Dad, "You don't have to pray if you don't want to." I was certain this was a foreign experience to him, and I didn't want him to feel uncomfortable. The voices grew nearer as our turn approached. My sister prayed that everyone would make good progress in treatment and we would learn to let go of our illnesses and trust God. Then I heard my dad's voice, low and gruff and grumbly and sweet: "Dear God, thank You for my girls. I love them more than words can say."

I had never heard my dad pray. It was like seeing a whole other side of something I already loved—like looking at the sunset, from above. And it made my year.

———

I learned a little something about mercy and forgiveness during Family Week. No one is perfect—not even our parents, whom we tend to see as infallible. They are human, and humans are a needy, sloppy, proud, stubborn bunch. All of us came from somewhere, and none of us came from perfection. It is important to afford our parents grace—at least as much or even more than we expect from them.

My parents loved me but seemed incapable of loving each other well. Relationships are sticky; things get in the way like doubt and mistrust and anger and rage and jealousy and pride and fear and blame. It happens. My parents came together long enough to create a life they would both value, and then they imploded. But I love them. We all did the best we could, and in some ways it was not enough. Whoever said our best would always be good enough was a liar. Sometimes it isn't. Sometimes we hurt one another, even those we love most, and sometimes some pretty heavy apologies are in order. I exchanged these with my family that week, and we all moved on.

Sometimes the healing is not so much in the hashing out as in the moving on.

God Whispers

*M*y family left at the end of August, and I settled into the routine—eat, cry, pout, pray, eat, cry, process, pray, eat—until a little dash of drama broke the monotony. On a hot morning in early September, I swallowed my cup of pills at the med window and shuffled into the dining hall, smiling hellos to staff and other residents. As I found my place at the breakfast table next to my friends, I knew instantly something was wrong. My usual "Mornin', y'all" was met with an awkward silence and sideways glances.

"What's with all of you?" I asked, forcing a smile. "Did someone die or something?"

"I sure hope not," Pippi drawled under her breath. Tiffany shushed her.

"What's going on?" I asked.

"She doesn't know?" Cora whispered to the group.

"Cora? Pip? *Know what?*"

Tiff reached across the table and put her cold hand over mine and said, "Honey, Nina is missing. She sneaked out between room checks overnight and never showed for weigh-in. Staff has been out searching all morning."

I turned to face Sharon, the MHT assigned to our table for breakfast. "Sharon? What, you guys just *lost* her?"

"They'll track her down, sweetie. Don't get yourself worked up," she said, noting the quiver of my chin. "Just pray. Don't worry; pray."

"I want to talk to Deb."

"You'll have your session this afternoon; for now, we have to trust the Lord with Nina."

My own indignation startled me, my face growing hot and my eyes welling with tears of an unfamiliar sort: anger.

"I want to talk to Deb—please."

"After breakfast."

"I'm not going to *eat* breakfast, and I need to talk to Deb, *please*."

I wasn't even sure why I so desperately wanted to talk with Deb; I hadn't exactly warmed to her, but I was angry with Staff for what I perceived as their collective incompetence, and since Deb was so insistent on my admitting my anger, I felt this was my chance to give her what she wanted. Sharon, who was immensely talented in dealing with every nuance of anorexic behavior, was not fazed by my tantrum. "Jena, you will see your therapist after lunch. Right now you need to eat your meal or you will be supplemented."

"I don't *need* to be supplemented; I am *fat*. You people expect us to trust you with our meal plans, trust you with our weight, trust you with our treatment, and I can't even trust you not to *lose* someone I care about!"

Girls at the other tables craned their necks to watch the drama unfold. I didn't care. I was upset, and for once I didn't mind anyone knowing it. Sharon continued encouraging me to eat, assuring me that Staff had everything under control. I sat, stony faced and flushed with stinging tears, and for the first time since I had arrived a month before, I refused to touch my meal.

"Jena, you are making a choice. If you choose not to eat your breakfast, you will make up the calories with the Ensure and you will receive an NC on your chart." NC was the dreaded red-ink notation indicating noncompliant behavior.

"And what does Nina get on her chart? Hmm? What, does she get an NC or an MIA?" Pippi tried to stifle a chuckle. "It's not funny, Pip! You don't know Nina's history. Until I know Nina is back here and hasn't done something horrible to herself, there is nothing funny about any of this!"

"Okay, Jen, we get it," Tiff said with exaggerated calm. Then she leaned over and whispered in my ear, "Just *eat* so you don't lose your level *again*."

I did not eat. I refused my meal, stood my ground, took my NC like a man. I sat at the table with Sharon for forty-five minutes after breakfast, sipping my compensatory cup of Ensure. It occurred to me in that moment, sitting at the table with my own private food warden, that all of this was slightly ridiculous. Why was I sitting in a treatment facility? Why was I so worried about a grown woman who happened to be out on the town unattended? Why was I refusing a plate of bacon frittata as though it were a bowl of rat poison? Why did I require a mental health technician to make sure I would consume twelve ounces of liquid nutrition? Why was I, at the spry young age of nineteen, wearing support hose to relieve my horrifically painful edema? Why was I, intelligent and full of promise, sequestered with these chapped, sullen, wasted rebels?

Because I myself was a chapped, sullen, wasted rebel and because I had put myself there.

———

Three hours later, two staff members walked through the double doors of the main lodge, Nina in tow. The Staff looked stern, relieved but clearly not amused, which was understandable. Nina, on the other hand, looked as though she were returning from a mountaintop expedition. She waved relaxed hellos to patients from across the room. I had been finishing some assigned reading when I looked up and saw her standing there, glistening with sweat and satisfaction.

"Where the heck have you been?" I asked, sounding like an overprotective parent.

"Oh, here and there," Nina replied with a dismissive wave of her hand. "I got a cup of coffee, I browsed in a hardware store, I bought a book and went to the park to read. No big deal."

"No big deal?" I echoed in disbelief. "Nina. You were a fugitive, for crying out loud. How long were you gone, anyway? What possessed you?"

Nina raked through her hair with her fingers and wiped the perspiration off her forehead. "I just needed a breather. I left at about four thirty, something like that. I took a little nap in the park. It was a good day."

I stared at her, shaking my head. "You are unbelievable, Nina. You had everyone worried sick. Did it even occur to you that we would worry?"

"I knew I'd be in trouble, yeah. But, I figured, whatever. I'm always in trouble for something." It was somewhat amusing to hear a thirty-two-year-old woman talking as though she were a twelve-year-old frequently grounded to her room.

"Well, yeah," I said. "You're going back on twenty-four-hour watch now. You can count on it."

Nina stood still for a moment, looked up, then back at me. "You know what, though?" she asked. "It doesn't matter. Today was really good for me."

Nina sat on the floor, leaning against the wall in the foyer. I sat beside her, not knowing what to think of my crazy, rebellious new friend. We were so different; if I had committed an act so rebellious as running away, I would have been a nervous wreck upon my return, like a dog with its tail between its legs. Nina seemed strangely refreshed. If I hadn't known better, I might have thought she'd been at a spa all morning.

"You know," she continued, her blue eyes shining, "God is pretty amazing. I felt Him with me everywhere I went today."

I was intrigued. Nina had not come to Remuda as a believer, and this was the first I had heard her speak about God. "Yeah?" I asked, eager to hear more.

"It was so weird. There's really not much to do in this town. I mean, there's the Remuda bookstore on the main road, and I would have liked to sit in there a while, but that would have been like turning myself in, so that was out. And there are only a few places to shop for clothes, but they're all Western stores, and that's not my thing."

"So you hung out in a hardware store?"

"Yes!" Nina laughed. "You'll never guess what I bought there." She rummaged in her canvas tote and retrieved a hardbound book written by Max Lucado, entitled *When God Whispers Your Name.*

"No way," I said. "You found that in a hardware store?"

"Yep," Nina said. "There was only one copy on the shelf, right by all these home improvement books. I swear God put it there just for me."

"That's pretty cool," I admitted. "So is it any good?"

"It was!" Nina smiled. "I read the whole thing, cover to cover, under a tree in the park."

I laughed out loud. "You crack me up, Nina. So you just camped out and read your book and then decided to come back?"

"Sort of," Nina said. "After a while, I needed a bathroom, so I walked up to this cute little house behind the main road and knocked on the door. A little old lady invited me in, and I used the bathroom and weighed myself. Then she gave me some iced tea—"

"Wait, wait, wait," I interjected. "Let me get this straight. You just went up to some random house and knocked? And you *weighed* yourself?" I chuckled at the absurdity.

"Yeah," Nina said, laughing along. "Crazy, huh? She was really sweet, the old lady. It was a pretty great day."

I repeated, "You weighed yourself."

"Yeah . . ." Nina said, trailing off. "It's getting up there, the number." I searched Nina's face for clues of how this made her feel. She was blank.

"So?" I asked, finally. "What does that mean for you?"

"You know what . . . ?" Nina began slowly, as though she were amazed at her own words. "I don't care as much as I thought I would. It just doesn't seem all that important. It seems kind of . . . stupid . . . all of a sudden. I mean, Jena, God dropped a book for me in the *hardware* store. And I had exactly enough cash in the pocket of my shorts to buy it. I'm telling you, it was the *only one* there."

"So what does that mean, you think?" I asked, bemused.

An expression of innocent wonder illuminated Nina's prematurely aged face. "It means . . . God is real. It means," Nina swallowed hard, tears glistening in her tired eyes. "It means He *knows* I'm *here.*"

I smiled at this new friend, for whom I was developing such a fondness. I patted Nina's bony knee as we sat beside each other on the floor. "He sure does."

It would be great if I could say that such a reminder was all we needed from God, and that Nina and I began running full speed toward health from that moment on. Nina, who subsequently lost all the privileges she had earned up until that day, did seem changed after her outing in the park. Nina met Jesus that day in August 1996 and began to latch onto a ladder of hope, beginning her slow climb, rung by rung. I, on the other hand, was beginning to see significant changes in my body at this time and was steadily outgrowing my clothes. This crisis, as can be imagined, was traumatic.

Not wanting to be faced each morning with the reminder of how much I had grown, I boxed up every pair of jeans and shorts I had brought with me—mostly size zeros, ones, and twos, and one pair of children's size fourteens—and gave them to Nina, who could still fit into some of them. I resigned myself to living in sweatpants and leggings, too ashamed to call home and ask my mother to send me bigger jeans.

My countenance changed with my body. I became increasingly depressed, despite the antidepressant and antianxiety meds I had been prescribed. My file relates notes from Nursing and the MHTs:

> Patient is quiet, waits now until conversation is initiated by others, is observing what peers are doing at mealtimes, eating more timidly, taking tiny bites, does not touch food to her lips, continue to monitor meals closely.

> Nursing reports Pt. becoming more tense at mealtimes. Speaks when spoken to only. Gradually increase Luvox for help with obsessions and compulsions.

> Pt. no longer presenting with superficially bright affect. Poor body image continues to be an issue. Very quiet, like processing something very intense, at times sad this a.m. Pt. states she has a lot on her mind.

> Unusually quiet at breakfast. States feeling tired and looks tired. Struggling through meals quietly. No disclosures. Tone of voice much quieter today. Less fastidious about her appearance. No makeup, wearing her glasses to meals. Eats very slowly.

It didn't take long for my treatment team to agree I needed extra attention in the area of body image improvement. *Expressing a great deal of body loathing,* my chart would read after the MHTs observed me. I needed an entire overhaul, and two group sessions a week with Julie, the body image therapist, were not going to cut it, and so she agreed to see me individually as well.

"I want you to write down three positive things that come to mind when you think of the word *fat*," Julie challenged me in our first one-on-one session.

"Do you mean body fat or dietary fat?" I asked, already fearing I wouldn't be able to do it.

"Either one," Julie said. "Just come up with three positive connotations of the word."

I struggled not to recoil from the word, shoved my notebook aside, and quit before I began. Finally I wrote in tiny, precise lettering, "protection." I was thinking of the chubby, rubbery legs of toddlers, and the bumps and bruises they seemed designed to withstand as they learned to walk.

Julie looked across the table, reading my answer upside down. "Good," she said. "Keep going."

I bit the end of my pencil, bobbing my knee like a hyperactive third-grader. I pondered a few minutes and came up blank. I set my pencil down on the table and looked up at Julie. "Sorry, I got nothin'."

"I'm sure you can think of something more," Julie said, furrowing her brow into a frown. "At least one. Try again."

"Julie," I said, shaking my head, "I'm telling you. I cannot come up with anything positive about this situation."

"What situation?"

My chin trembled and I rolled my eyes, embarrassed. "*This* situation," I said, gesturing toward my own body. "I'm a cow," I said, my voice barely a whisper.

"But you're not," Julie replied, as though it were the truth.

"According to you," I retorted. "How do I know I can believe you? Is anyone ever going to clue me in on how much I've gained? Do I *ever* get to know the weight of *my own body*?"

"I don't think that would be such a good idea right now," Julie said, smiling sweetly. "Do you?"

"I'm freaking out, Julie," I cried.

"I know," she said. "It will get better."

"When?"

Julie switched gears, ignoring my question. "I'm gonna give you a little assignment," she said, scribbling something on her notepad. "I want you to take a half an hour each day to get away by yourself and spend some time just talking to God. I want you to tell Him everything you're feeling about your 'situation.' Start today."

"How am I supposed to get half an hour to go anywhere alone?" I asked. "Isn't that against the rules?"

Julie winked at me. "I have some pull around here."

———

I used my new unaccompanied free time each day to do as Julie said: I got away by myself to get honest before God. At first I felt awkward, not knowing how to fill thirty minutes. Eventually, though, as I gained weight and grew more and more frustrated, I began to experience some relief—and release— from my solitary moments in God's presence.

Group therapy was making a difference, too, as formulaic and cliché as some of the approaches seemed at first; slowly I became less eager to scoff with my more cynical peers at the positive affirmations and "healthy speak." I even joined in with some of the younger patients as they scribbled key phrases on their notebooks and the soles of their shoes: "I am more than my body!" "I deserve to be well!" "I am God's workmanship!"

Positive thinking may have gotten a bad reputation in recent years by some of the more self-important and prideful figures in our media, but there is something to it. Scripture tells us that "as a man thinks in his heart, so is he"; our thoughts define our human experience, to a great degree. A motivational sign hangs in the office of a friend of mine, a bright photo of a distance runner in action, his entire muscular body beaded with sweat. The caption reads, "Whether you think you can or you think you can't, you're right." I have come to see some truth in that bold statement.

What I learned at Remuda, though, went beyond mere positive thinking. It went further than the logic of facts. The facts were important—for example, "My body requires food for energy"—but more crucial than the facts was the truth. With the skilled and compassionate counsel of the Staff, we scoured our Bibles for truths that were especially applicable to our struggles and that precisely shot down the lies we had come to believe. Day after day, we devoured the Word of God, artistically displaying our finds on poster boards and construction paper, taping them to the doors of our rooms, the walls above our beds. God's words were everywhere, for all to see in puff paint and permanent marker:

"God has planned a hopeful future for me!"
(Jeremiah 29:11)

"I cast all my cares upon the Lord, for He cares for me!"
(1 Peter 5:7)

"Nothing is impossible with God."
(Luke 1:37)

Hollow

The Word of God is powerful, cutting through even the thickest skin on the most jaded cynic. We tried at first, many of us, to pretend it wasn't getting in. But self-contempt and self-hatred can only thrive so long in the glorious revealing light of the truth. There were those among us who managed to stave off the positive influence of our surroundings, but they truly had to fight against it. They had to make the conscious choice to remain shackled in darkness. Sadly, a few of my peers made that choice and stuck to it.

Watching these rejections was painful, but it was also an important lesson in free will. We cannot force others to believe what we want them to believe or do what we want them to do.

A month and a half into treatment, something truly horrifying happened. I awakened one morning at six o'clock to make my way to the nurses' station for weigh-in, and as I climbed the dusty hill to the main lodge, a sharp, empty sort of twisting pain arose from the pit of my stomach. The pain, I noted in disbelief, came with a voice—a thundering, rumbling sort of gurgle that announced itself with a proud crescendo.

My stomach growled.

My body actually had the nerve—the audacity!—to *ask* for food in the morning, as if it had learned to *expect* it. I was terrified. I was embarrassed. And I was angry.

"This is good, you know," Nina said as I sat beside her on a bench outside the main hall before breakfast. "This is what is supposed to happen. This means you are—*we* are—becoming normal again."

"I know, Nin," I whined. "That's the scary part! I'm not ready to be normal. I'm not done needing to be sick, you know?"

Nina drew a line in the dusty ground with the toe of her white canvas oxford. "Yeah, I understand that part."

"I mean, what if I can never go back? What if I can't hack recovery, and I want to go back to being sick and then I can't? What if I just totally lose control? What if I let myself go?"

Nina grinned absently, still staring at her toe circling in the dust. "That sounds kind of nice, actually—letting yourself go. It sounds freeing, like letting yourself off the hook."

"I'm scared of that kind of freedom, I think."

"Me, too," Nina admitted.

"I don't trust myself at all anymore," I said.

"So trust God instead," Nina replied simply, then shifted her stare from her feet to my eyes and grinned.

"Listen to you!" I said, punching Nina in the arm playfully. "Was that *hope* I just heard in your voice?"

"Shh," Nina teased. "Don't tell anybody."

Spiritually, things were looking up. Watching God at work in people does something to a person. You cannot deny what is happening right before your eyes. There is no greater miracle than the transformation of a heart, from lover of self to lover of God, and I was watching it happen all around me.

The spirit of God was—and is—at work at Remuda Ranch. To behold the spiritual transformation of some of those around me, like Nina, was to behold the power of truth. To behold the devastation that had brought us all to this place was to behold the power of the lie.

Our job was to choose between the two.

Life on the Inside

t is amazing how quickly and seamlessly one can adjust to life within the confines of a mental institution. Those things that at first were so disturbing—the random screams and shrieks; the tendency of some residents to disassociate into catatonia for an hour or so at random; the seemingly intellectual, well-dressed grown women wont to burst into tears over an extra pat of butter on their meal trays; the seemingly unprovoked outbursts, such as that of an especially volatile patient named Ellen, whose rage erupted at a pregnant MHT whom she pushed to the floor—become old hat before too long. For the most part, treatment felt like being away at an all-girls Bible camp—an all-girls Bible camp full of extremely sick and disturbed campers.

There were some light moments. There was the day a group of us stood in the foyer, many still quite frail-looking, and turned to find a lost-looking couple of senior citizens standing just inside the front doors to the main lodge. They wore cameras around their necks and floral-printed shirts, and the woman took in the sight of us, gasped, and said to the man at her side, "Oh, Harold, I don't think *this* is the bed-and-breakfast!"

The days were neatly organized and scheduled, with precise time slots for breakfast, chapel, snack, didactics, lunch, therapy, group, snack, dinner, free time or movie time, art therapy or movement class or spiritual growth or relapse prevention, snack, free time, bed. I enjoyed the predictability, having become less and less able to handle change the sicker I got. Having become increasingly obsessive as our illnesses progressed, most of us yearned for structure to confine us and keep us from spilling out of the safety zone. We complained, of course, because to admit that we relished the militant itinerary would have been an admission of our complete inability to cope with the chaos inherent to real life, on the outside.

The safety net didn't last long, however. One sweltering Tuesday morning, Deb pulled the rug out from under our routine. I knew something was up when I saw her standing by the front doors to the dining hall instead of our usual meeting place at the rear door. She had that look in her wild brown eyes. I *hated* that look.

"Whoa, what are you doing all the way over here?" I asked as I approached her, carrying my journal and books. "I feel like a dog whose water dish has been moved."

"Change of plans," she replied, wild eyes aflame. "We're going to do a little field work." She led me out the main doors into the blazing hot sunlight.

"Field work?" I echoed. I followed her, dreading whatever scheme she had devised. I grew more anxious as we were walked so far we had nearly left the campus and wandered into open desert.

"Deb, um, you're not kidnapping me, are you?"

"Maybe," she said breathlessly, wiping sweat from her forehead.

I rolled my eyes. I hated it when she tried to be cute.

"Okay," Deb said finally. "This should be a good spot."

"For what?" I demanded to know.

"For you to free yourself."

"Excuse me?" I asked, half hoping she was turning me loose, like someone who finds a wild animal and returns it to its natural habitat.

"I sense so much unreleased anger in you, Jena," Deb confronted me as she squinted, shielding her eyes from the blinding noonday sun with her cupped hand. "I don't know yet what it's all about, but it's there. And I wonder even if you are unable to put words to it yet if you might be able to release some of it out here, safely away from everyone else."

"Release it how?" I asked, already growing more annoyed.

"I want you," she began, squeezing my shoulders for emphasis, "just to go ahead and *scream*."

"What?" I laughed in disbelief. "You must be joking!"

"No joke. I want you to scream—as loud as you want, for as long as you want."

"And what if I don't want to?"

Deb stared at me a moment. I assumed it was her attempt at a dramatic pause. "Do it anyway."

I laughed haughtily at the absurdity. "This is insane," I said. "I don't scream. This is just not me. You're asking me to do something dishonest."

"How do you know?" Deb countered. "Do you really know what is and is not 'you' anymore?"

"Deb!" I protested, beginning to cry. "I'm sorry, okay? I just can't."

Deb let me cry. "Jena, I think you *can* do what I'm asking. You just don't *want* to."

"I'm not angry, though, Deb," I insisted. "I mean, I'm a lot of things: I'm sad, I'm scared, I'm frustrated, I'm just plain screwed up in the head. I'm all kinds of crazy, but I just don't feel that I am angry. I'm sorry."

"You're feeling frustrated, Jena?"

"Yes."

"With what?" Deb asked, squinting against the light.

"I don't know . . . with myself, I guess."

"And with me, probably."

"Probably," I conceded.

"Well, guess what? I'm feeling frustrated with you, too." Deb laid the words out there in the middle of the desert and let them lie a while, sizzling in the sand. I waited for her to justify her statement, back it up with some overdue disclaimer to soften the blow, but she did not. Apparently, it was a stand-alone sentiment.

"I'm sorry," I said, as a default response.

Deb kicked at a twig on the ground. "I'm sorry, too." And with that, she headed back to the Ranch.

"I am so frustrated!" I grunted, as I paced Nina's bunkhouse bedroom. "I don't know what she wants from me! Why is this so important to her? I swear, she must be eligible for some kind of bonus check if she gets me to scream. I am on the brink, Nin; this woman is gonna be the end of me, I'm telling you."

"I know," Nina nodded. "I'm frustrated, too. I'm going stir crazy. I gotta get out of here. I can't take it anymore; I'm gonna lose what's left of my sanity, I swear."

I looked at Nina, sitting Indian-style on her bed in the bunkhouse. She had that twinkle in her blue eyes—that glimmer of mischief I had come to love about her. I flopped down beside her on my stomach, tucking her big stuffed dog under my chin. "Okay, let's go," I teased. "Let's hop a plane to Vegas. I have four dollars; that ought to get us there, right?"

"I mean it," Nina said, her eyes wide as she swept her short auburn hair across her forehead. "I have to get out, at least for a little while." She glanced out the window, then back at me, and bit her bottom lip as though to stifle a Cheshire cat smile. "Wanna go on a field trip?"

"You're not serious."

Nina's sunken cheeks filled out slightly as her grin widened. "I'm totally serious. Don't I look serious?"

"You do—that's what scares me."

She lowered her voice to a conspiratorial whisper. "You're done with your one-on-one, right?"

"Yeah . . ."

"And you're not expected at med window until after dinner, right?"

"Right . . ."

"Already weighed in, already done with group?"

"Uh-huh . . ."

"Me, too!" That seemed to settle it. She sprang up, her sticklike arms spread wide. "Let's break out!"

I laughed. "Just where are we going, Houdini?"

"Anywhere! The mall. Let's take a cab out of town." She was the picture of wily glee, energy electrifying her tiny body as she rummaged in the side table drawer beside her bed.

"What are you looking for, your car keys?" I joked as I watched, my curiosity piqued.

"Not exactly." She emerged with a yellow business card: the holy grail. "Aha!"

I leaned over to read the card. "Dial-a-Ride? Where did you get this?"

"Does it matter?"

I giggled, my heart fluttering at the thought of being caught committing such an act of noncompliance. "I guess not!"

"Okay, here's the plan," Nina said, her authoritative

personality coming to the fore. "We'll run up to the main lodge and ask for access to our bins. We have to have a reason, so we'll say we want to shave our legs. When they give us our bins, we'll grab our razors, but we'll also pocket our cash and credit cards. Then we'll go to the sinks to shave, but I'll finish first and turn my things back in, and ask for the phone to call home, but really I'll call for our ride, then I'll very discreetly head out front. You'll stall a few minutes, turn in your things, and come meet me."

I could not contain my amusement. "You've given this some thought."

"Just a little," Nina grinned. "So? Whaddya think? I mean, what's the worst that could happen?"

I wavered. "Well . . ."

"Come on," she probed. "Am I the only one getting claustrophobic in this joint? I don't think so. So let's go AWOL! It'll be good for you!"

She was right. I had always been obsessively compliant, and this would be a welcome break from my voluntary confinement to the rules. Within an hour, we were giggling nervously in the back of a cab as the Ranch grew distant through the back window.

This day in the history of my life has become one of my fondest memories. A favorite photo shows Nina standing on an escalator in the mall, eyes closed, laughing hysterically, her veiny hand gripping a green styrofoam cup of Gloria Jean's gourmet coffee: our favorite forbidden fruit. I don't remember buying anything other than the coffee, but I remember laughing harder than I had in months and feeling a strong sense of sisterhood with Nina. For the first time in over a year, we felt alive. We felt normal.

Then we took a cab back to Remuda and faced our consequences. In the cab, we discussed the fact that neither of us had eaten since morning snack at 10:30, and it was by then well after dinnertime. In a strange display of sudden self-respect and responsibility, we decided we would make up the calories when we returned to the Ranch.

Forty-five minutes later, we walked through the double doors into the main lodge and were greeted with relieved hugs from residents and stern scoldings from Staff. We were told that punitive action would be taken, but that it would be decided by our case therapists the following morning. So we made our way into the kitchen and prepared our long overdue meal, a curious platter of new favorites: vanilla yogurt, granola, pears, and cottage cheese.

The next morning at our community meeting, Nina and I compared notes regarding the corrective measures we had been dealt. Nina, as we expected, was pushed back a level and denied her privilege to afternoon walks. I, on the other hand, was congratulated and promoted a level, and—ironically—taken off of building restriction. Deb felt it was good for me to stretch a little and dare to be imperfect.

Nina and I shared a good laugh over the whole thing, and then we prepared to return to the daily grind of intensive therapy and processing groups—the tears, the anger, the screaming, the fits, the threats, the occasional breakthrough, the odd epiphanies.

But something had shifted in my approach to myself after that forbidden day out. I had managed to chisel a small crack into the corner of the thin, soundproof glass that separated me from the rest of the world. Not enough to escape, but enough that I could return later and chip away more and more, if the spirit moved me, and if I dared.

The Art of Being

*E*ach morning breakfast at the Ranch was followed by a community chapel service in the main lodge, during which we would sing and pray and participate in a short Bible lesson applicable to our quest for recovery. I loved this part of the day, because I got to sing, and eventually I was asked to play the piano on occasion. I was in my element when making music. It helped me forget that my body felt like it was no longer my own, controllable and obedient and starved into submission. When I was singing and playing, I was distracted from the feeling of food in my stomach and the way the waistband of my pants was beginning to bite into my fleshy belly. I was grateful for this distraction, though it only lasted for an hour a day.

Deb, however, felt differently.

"Jena," she called after me as I left chapel one morning, "can I speak with you a minute?"

I backed up. "What's up?"

"You sounded lovely this morning; thank you for sharing your music."

"Oh. Um . . ." I stammered, not trusting the look in Deb's eyes. "Thank you?"

"You knew there was more, huh?" she asked, winking at me. She seemed to think she was being cute. I, feeling threatened already, was not amused.

"I assumed so."

"I'd like you to stop playing the piano for a few weeks."

"Okay," I replied, perturbed. "For chapel, or at any time?"

"Altogether," she said authoritatively. "I'd like you to stop playing altogether. Just for a few weeks."

"Tsssk," I breathed, looking away. "Why?"

"I don't think it serves our purpose right now in therapy," Deb said. "I know you're not happy about it, and that's okay. You can be angry with me if you want to."

"I'm not angry," I said quickly. I didn't want to get into this discussion while the other patients bustled about within earshot.

"Well," Deb chuckled, "I'm not done yet."

"Oh, joy," I said sarcastically. "What else?"

Deb grinned, enjoying the uneasy suspense she was creating. "I don't want you to sing, either."

"Oh, come *on*," I blurted. "Why *not*, for heaven's sake?"

"It just doesn't serve our purpose together now, Jena."

"What the heck does that mean?"

Deb smiled. "I understand you're angry, but there is no need to get defensive."

"I'm *not angry*!" I said. "I just don't understand. Why are you punishing me?"

"We'll talk more about this in our session this afternoon," Deb said. "You need to get to your group now."

"Yeah, but Deb, can't you just—"

"Jena," Deb said, speaking as though I were four. "Get to your group now. We'll process this later."

"I can't wait," I said, turning on my heel.

That afternoon, I curled into a tight ball on the couch in Deb's office, wrapped up in my thick sweatshirt, both in an effort to keep warm and to protect myself from our impending confrontation.

"Okay, go ahead," Deb said, getting comfortable in her chair. "Tell me how angry you are with me."

"You'd like that, wouldn't you?" I retorted, playing with the cuff of my sleeve.

"Why do you think that?" Deb asked, playing dumb.

"Because you seem stuck on this idea of getting me to admit I am angry."

"Ah," Deb nodded. "Yes, I do think that will be an important moment for you."

"Deb," I said, "seriously. For the millionth time this week, I am not angry. Okay? That's not my problem."

"Hmm," Deb said.

"What, you don't believe me? Why would I lie, Deb? How is that helping me?"

"What scares you about being angry?"

"You're assuming I'm scared now!" I said, growing exasperated. "Man! Can't I ever just be allowed to decide how I'm feeling without you telling me how I'm feeling?"

Deb smiled. "Of course, Jena. How are you feeling?"

"Confused! Why am I not allowed to sing? Why can't I play the piano? What does it mean when you say those things don't 'serve our purpose' in therapy? What *is* our purpose in therapy?"

Deb nodded. "What do you think it is?"

"I have *no idea*, Deb!" I said, beginning to cry. "All I know is I must be missing the point, because I am not getting anything out of this, and I feel like I am no good at it!"

"No good at what?" Deb asked.

"Therapy!" I shrieked. "I stink at therapy! I'm wasting your time, my time, thousands of dollars . . . I just want to go home!"

"What would you do at home to stay in recovery?"

"I don't know," I said. "Take a break. Spend more time with God. Journal more. I don't know."

"That reminds me," Deb said, pointing her finger. "I'd like you to take the next week off from journaling."

"What?"

"No journaling, no writing," Deb repeated. "Just for this week."

"Deb, what the *heck?*"

"Please don't yell at me."

"Sorry! But what is going *on*, Deb? Are you *trying* to drive me crazy? I can't sing, I can't play piano, and now I can't *write?*"

"Jena," Deb said, clasping her hands between her knees, "I want you to just *be* for a while."

"Just . . . be?" I echoed.

"Yes. Stop doing, and just be. You are not a human doing, you are a human being, and I am afraid you don't know how to stop doing, to stop performing. So I am enforcing a time of rest."

"Enforcing a time of . . . Oh, Deb. Don't do this," I pleaded. "Please. Okay?"

"You are not to read or write or sing or play the piano or draw—"

"No art, either? For how long?"

"A week. I think you can handle that."

"I'll go crazy! What will I do?"

"Nothing!"

"I can't do nothing, Deb. I would feel so . . ."

"So what? You would feel so what?"

"Lazy. Useless."

"What else?"

I was silent.

Deb continued, "How would your self-perception of laziness and uselessness make you feel?"

"Ashamed."

"What else?"

"Guilty."

"Mmm," Deb said. "When you feel those things—the guilt, the shame, the sense of uselessness—is someone to blame for causing you to feel that way?"

"Of course not," I said, quick to defend whatever nameless outsider I feared she might be attempting to incriminate. "It's all my fault."

"How does that make you feel toward yourself?"

I threw my head back and drew in a sharp breath. "Angry!"

Deb stared at me intently while I refused to meet her eyes. Finally, she spoke in an exaggeratedly soft, collected tone. "And that is why I want you to stop doing these extra activities. You have become an expert at distracting yourself to keep from feeling unpleasant emotions. When you are out of the hospital, you distract yourself with starvation and the abuse of your body. Now that you are in treatment and starvation and abuse as coping mechanisms are no longer an option, you distract yourself with other things. They are all good things—journaling and art and music and ministry, they're all good in and of themselves—but you are abusing them, just as you abused your body. You cannot do that anymore."

"But what will happen if I can't distract myself?" I asked, through the flood of tears that had burst loose from the dam of my emotional hypercontrol.

"The feelings will come."

"They're not good feelings," I sobbed.

"I know," she said. "But you need to let them come anyway.

You'll feel them, and we'll process them and pray through them, and they'll pass. Then you can heal and get on with your life."

I let the tears roll down my cheeks without bothering to wipe them away. I felt suddenly exhausted.

"Jena," Deb said, "they're only emotions. Emotions cannot kill you."

"It's not dying I'm afraid of," I said. "It's the emotions I'm afraid of!"

"I know," Deb nodded. "But distracting yourself from them is never going to make them go away. You've got to feel them. It's the only way through the jungle."

I sighed and fell back into the couch cushions. "Can't I just set up camp in the jungle instead?"

Deb laughed. "You'll get mighty bored in the jungle without your journal and your piano and your singing."

"So you're seriously doing this. You are seriously banning me from all the things I enjoy," I said, still in disbelief.

"I seriously am," Deb said. "It's not a punishment, Jena. It's an assignment."

"No," I protested. "An assignment would imply that you were giving me something to do. You are forbidding me to do anything!"

Deb grinned, clearly amused. "The irony is delightful, isn't it?"

I stared her down. If she really wanted me to feel and express my anger, she may just have to be my first victim.

The following week was horrible. I went to group, listened to other girls share their horrendous stories of abuse and tragedy. But this week was different. Before I had listened and I had nodded and cooed and said, "Oh, I'm so sorry" and hugged them and prayed with them and for them, but I had not cried. I had often felt guilty for sitting in a group full of weeping women without shedding a single tear, though my heart ached for them. This week, though, with my journal locked away in a bin and without the release of making music, something snapped. *Everything* made me cry. I felt as though the tears would never dam, that I would die this way, perhaps that very night—a victim of drowning in my own bed, tears choking the very life out of me as I sank into my pillow, sobbing and mute.

Of course, Deb saw this as a breakthrough. I seemed to be making up for lost time, for all the years I had spent over-controlling my emotions. It seemed as if all the tears usually cried in early childhood through adolescence and young adulthood had been saved up and concentrated and were finally exploding from my eyes. The problem was, I had no idea what they meant or what they were about.

In group session after group session that week I sat, soggy and sloppy and sobbing quietly to myself. As always, each group would open with a feelings check-in. Deb or another therapist would ask what I was feeling, and I would shrug. It seemed I no longer had the capacity to formulate sentences. I felt like a prisoner in a cage of silent tears. I remember glancing across the room and meeting Andrea's eyes, suddenly feeling a strong bond with the silent, willowy figure in the corner. I understood her silence, just then. Sometimes life just seems too complicated a sport in which to participate; sometimes language just seems to fall short of expression. Sometimes it's all just too much, too soon, too hard, too scary, too risky. And so we opt out. We shut off and power down, with an almost audible *click*.

I shut off that week, refused to speak or share or pray—not out of stubbornness, but because I had nothing to share but tears. After a few days, the other patients and the techs seemed to accept my weepiness as the way things were going to be for a while. No one bothered me; no one asked what was wrong.

I can only imagine what the new residents must have thought. "What's with the downer curled up on the couch?" they might have asked. "Oh, her," the others might have said. "That's Jena; don't mind her. She just cries. It's what she does."

It felt as though I would cry forever.

———

I had grown used to writing out prayers to God during my free time during the day between sessions. Of course, what I did not realize was that, by writing them out, my prayers had become more and more eloquent and less and less honest and organic and sincere. Prayer, for me, had become akin to poetry, to art. It's no wonder I felt I had stagnated in my relationship to Christ; God does not desire eloquence and frills. He wants intimacy; He wants our hearts and all that is in them, as dark and messy and imperfect as they may be.

It was becoming clear that everything—everything—was now completely out of my control. I could not control my body, which was expanding and becoming soft and curvy and feminine and unruly and disobedient to my wishes. I could not control my food intake, which had been increased to who knows how many calories per day. I could not control my emotions, which had manifested as a never-ending tidal wave of tears. I could not control what others thought of me—not Robyn and the others in group who thought I was phony and superficial; not Deb, who thought I was angry and repressed and unwilling to work and yield to her counsel; not the new patients, who probably thought I was a certifiable basket case. And now I could no longer control my prayers, could no longer keep them neat and tidy and polite and reverent and pious. Instead, they became silent screams for mercy.

I went outside one afternoon to my little place on the bench at the top of a dusty hill overlooking the desert. Having no journal, I began to speak my prayers aloud for the first time. "God, are You even there? Do You even care that my life is in the toilet, that I have no future, no control, no desire to fight anymore? Is this what You want for me? Why am I here? What happened to my life? What happened to me? I used to be the girl everyone believed in, who everyone thought would go on to do such wonderful things . . . and look where I am now: I'm a total mental case, sucking up thousands of dollars in treatment costs, wasting her life. How can You love me? *Do* You love me? Why did You create me in the first place, if You knew I was just going to defect on You like this? I need to start all over again, I need another shot at life. But I don't want it. I'm nineteen years old, and I am exhausted. I just want to be done. I'm tired," I sobbed. "I'm just so tired."

I sobbed and sobbed, not knowing what else to do. In the past, when hit with a flood of emotion so strong, I would have wrapped my fingers around my bony arm, letting my thinness comfort me. This would no longer work. My fingers would no longer reach all the way around my upper arm, which was now filled out. I could have tried to find another stone to rub against my hand, to sand down the skin and watch the blood flow, but I just didn't have the energy. And, I thought to myself, even if I did, what would that prove?

My Bible was beside me on the bench, and I stared at it for what seemed like forever before mustering the strength to flip it open. Carelessly, I flipped to somewhere in the middle, not bothering to look at what book I had landed in. I wasn't sure I even had the energy to read, but suddenly a passage seemed to leap off the page: *The Lord will guide you always; he will satisfy your needs in a sun-scorched land and will strengthen your frame* (Isaiah 58:11).

I couldn't believe my eyes. I had never even noticed this passage before, and it was as though it had been written in my Bible that afternoon, a personal note from my Father to me. I needed guidance more than anything, and here it was, promised to me in Scripture. God was promising to "satisfy my needs"—even though I did not know what my needs were—"in a sun-scorched land." Looking around me, I laughed out loud. I was sitting in the middle of the Sonoran Desert. How cool that God knew exactly where I would be when I read that passage. Furthermore, God had promised to "strengthen (my) frame." I was ambivalent, at best, about that part. I still wasn't sure I wanted my "frame" to be "strengthened"—and yet I was sure there was no such Scripture that said, "I will make you skin and bone and give you my blessing to be an invalid."

Suddenly inspired to hear more from the Spirit of God, I flipped to one of my favorite passages in His word, Jeremiah 29:11, which reads, "'For I know the plans I have for you,' declares the Lord, 'plans to prosper you and not to harm you, plans to give you hope and a future.'" I read those words over and over and over again, weeping in that "sun-scorched land." I felt a wave of peace wash over me as I realized I had never been the one in control, anyway. God was. It didn't matter if my plans for my life had failed; God had plans of His own for me. It didn't matter if I was bad at therapy and couldn't identify my issues and my needs; God knew my needs better than anyone, and He had promised to satisfy them. It didn't matter if I felt as though I had lost all hope and could see no future for myself, because I was beginning to believe that God Himself would give me hope *and* a future.

My part of the deal was to trust Him and stick around for it.

Changing of the Guard

*O*nce a week, after breakfast and chapel, patients attended Team Meeting, where each patient sat in a circle in a private room with her therapist, psychologist, psychiatrist, Staff representatives from Nursing and Dietary, Jody the nutritionist, and the MHTs. The meetings were brief—maybe ten minutes for each patient—and mainly served as check points to make sure everyone was on the same page. At these meetings patients were granted passes, given praise or constructive criticism, and promoted or demoted on the level system. My Team Meetings, until this point, had been uneventful, save for the day I was promoted following the breakout with Nina. One Team Meeting, though, at the end of September, changed everything.

I walked into the conference room in the main lodge, said hello, and noticed there was one face missing from the circle: my therapist.

"Where's Deb?" I asked no one in particular.

"How are things going for you, Jena?" asked Dr. Hall.

"Not bad. Where's Deb?" I repeated.

"I meant how are things going, with you and Deb? How do you feel your therapy is progressing?"

I chuckled to myself, catching on. "She dumped me, didn't she?"

"Of course not," one of the nurses chimed in. "But we're interested in hearing your thoughts on this. Are you comfortable with how things are going between you and Deb?"

No, I thought. *But that may be because I can't stand the woman.* "I guess, I mean, sort of. Not really. I don't know. Why?"

"Well," Dr. Hall began, "you've been here close to four months. Now would generally be the time we would begin talking about releasing you or sending you on to our transitional living program in Chandler. But . . ."

"But I'm only a level two," I said. "Because I stink at this."

"At what?" an MHT asked.

I laughed. "Treatment, apparently!"

There were smiles around the room. Dr. Hall spoke first. "You don't stink at treatment. People don't generally fail at a treatment program, but sometimes that treatment program can fail the patient. We want to be sure that doesn't happen to you."

"So . . . what? Obviously, you're not releasing me yet."

"No," Dr. Hall said, smiling. "We'd like to see you stay here one more month, and we think it's best to assign you a different therapist."

Yes! I thought. "But what will Deb think?"

"Deb is aware of the new plan," Sharon the MHT assured me.

"So she *did* dump me!" I laughed.

Deb and the team had decided my progress under Deb's wing was, shall we say, disappointing. Therapists are like shoes: if there is not a good fit, things can be downright uncomfortable. This was the case with Deb and me. It's not that she was a "bad" therapist or I was a "bad" patient, though I did battle that notion for a time; our personalities simply were not well suited enough for any lasting fruit to be born of our therapeutic endeavor together.

Enter Mark, a handsome, graying middle-aged man—the quintessential "psychologist" stereotype, the sort one might expect to play Freud in some cheesy movie-of-the-week. Mark, at the time, was Remuda's token male therapist. If I had been unsure of Deb's expert knowledge of eating disorders, I was about to encounter her polar opposite: Mark knew his subject intuitively, and his uncanny ability to get inside my troubled little head would prove most uncomfortable. I both needed and feared such an intrusion.

Mark met me at the main lodge on the day of our first session, just after breakfast on a Monday morning. He was tall and had impeccable posture. I remember feeling small beside him as we walked down the dusty hill to his office in one of the rustic outbuildings.

There I woodenly positioned myself across from him, and he pulled his chair up to sit barely three feet in front of me. He looked me squarely in the eye and said, "You look terrified."

"Do I?" I asked, pulling my hands into my sleeves because Mark, like Deb, was apparently also a huge fan of a freezing cold office. "I'm sorry."

"Well, you don't have to be sorry," he laughed softly as he rested his elbows on his knees. "If you are terrified, then I appreciate you looking terrified. You're being honest with me already."

"I guess."

"So then, you are scared?"

"Maybe, a little."

"Why, do you suppose? You've been here for several months. One might say that the hard part is over. You've been through a lot of changes in the past hundred and twenty days."

"You mean I've gained weight," I frowned, fighting back tears.

Excruciating silence, as the echo of my words hung like a fog in the cold, tiny office.

"It's difficult for you to verbalize that." He wasn't asking a question; he knew. I nodded, unable to maintain eye contact. More silence. The tears were flowing, defenseless against Mark's penetrating gaze.

I glanced up, hoping to find a box of tissue on the table beside me. There was none. Reading my mind, Mark pulled a tiny package of Kleenex out of his shirt pocket. I laughed at his intuitive response and reached out my hand. To my surprise, he pulled a Kleenex from the package, leaned forward, and held it to my nose.

"Blow," he said, gently.

I laughed again, his hand still holding the tissue to my nose. "Are you serious?"

"Blow," he repeated, matter-of-factly.

I blew my nose, ever so gingerly, through an awkward giggle.

"I'll bet it's been a while since somebody wiped your nose for you."

"Oh, about sixteen years," I said.

"How does it feel?"

"Bizarre." I was shaking my head, wondering what this strange man was up to.

"Why should it feel bizarre to accept care from another person?"

"Because I'm not a toddler, for starters."

"Do you have to be a toddler to be cared for, or to need care?"

I leaned back in my chair and stared at Mark, holding my crumpled Kleenex to my face. I didn't seem able to answer his question.

"You are going to *have* to accept care from me, Jena, and it is going to feel bizarre, probably for quite some time. But it is the only way we are going to get you through this new crisis of wellness. You'll have to forgive me," Mark continued. "A moment ago I mentioned your already going through the hard part. The truth is, *this* is the hard part. Frostbite hurts the most as it thaws. Broken bones ache when they begin to fuse back together. Anorexia is most painful when you cannot necessarily *see it* anymore. I understand that, and if you'll let me, I am going to help you through the hardest part of your recovery."

"I just don't know if I want it," I whispered.

"You're not sure you want my help?"

"No, recovery. I don't know if I want recovery."

Mark smiled, rubbing his beard. "Then that's where we'll start."

___

The man, in my opinion, was brilliant. Mark at that time had nearly twenty years of experience in treating eating disorders. Deb's seemingly scripted sessions had annoyed me, and often I had not taken her seriously. With Mark, I had the sense I was sitting with an old friend—or, maybe, the wise father of an old friend. His counsel was firm, truthful, biblical, and consistent; and his tone was causal and direct. He gradually helped me believe that the words *life* and *anorexia* were mutually exclusive. Ultimately, I could not have them both. I *wanted* them both, and therein lay my dilemma. I had to choose, and I did not feel prepared to make that choice.

"What if I could be successful going on the way I was, just to a lesser degree?"

"The way you were? You mean when you had one foot in the grave last July?"

"That's an exaggeration," I answered back.

"Let's be frank," he said. "When you arrived here four months ago, your body was shutting down, your organs were consuming themselves for energy, you were severely dehydrated, and you were abusing a pharmacy full of medications—but *you* think maybe you could live successfully that way, if given another shot at it."

"Well, maybe I don't have to be quite that low," I countered, returning to the familiar, safe area of numbers. "Maybe I could accept a slightly higher weight."

"A menstruating weight, you mean?"

"Maybe."

"*Maybe?*" He looked at me as though I had three heads. "Do you *want* osteoporosis?"

"No."

"Do you want to have children one day?"

"Yes."

"Do you want to continue feeling exhausted and depressed from being out of whack hormonally?"

"Not really."

"So you want to maintain a menstruating weight, then. And what weight would you be comfortable maintaining?"

"I don't know . . . as long as it's under a hundred pounds, I guess I'd be comfortable."

"Not for long. At even ninety-nine pounds, Jena, a woman of your build is underweight. I doubt you would have a period at ninety-nine pounds. You would be cold all of the time, and you would once again begin to shut down metabolically."

"But I remember how I *felt* at that weight. I felt *fine*."

"Baloney. Then why did you continue to restrict your calories? Why did you have to lose another twenty pounds? Why not stop there, if you felt so great?"

I picked at my cuticles and looked away. After a moment, I shrugged and said, "I guess I still felt fat."

"Of course you did. You were utterly delusional."

"Oh Mark, you say the sweetest things," I teased.

"And let me remind you that fat is not a feeling, by the way."

"Ugh, I hate it when you say that," I whined.

"Yeah, well here's another one you're not going to like: you were incompetent."

"Not really," I protested. "I was still going to school at a hundred pounds, still working and singing and playing, doing all of my normal activities."

"Eating more than a couple hundred calories a day is a normal activity. You weren't doing that, were you?"

"No."

"Well," he said nonchalantly, "What do *you* call your inability to eat? I call it a major incompetence."

"But I wasn't *dying*."

"Baloney."

He was right. I was tired of fighting his logic, and he wasn't going to let up. I don't know what I expected him to say. Perhaps I hoped he would pat me on the head and send me off with his blessing to live a semidisordered existence. Instead, he told me the truth: there was no such option.

I started to cry. "When does the fear go away?"

"The fear of . . . ?"

"Of living without my disorder. Of letting go."

"The fear only goes away *as* you do it. Not before. I won't lie to you," he warned, "it will probably be terrifying for a good long time. But your heavenly Father will lead you through it, and you'll do it *through* the fear. And your support circle will hold you up until you can stand on your own. It will take everything you have—all of your resolve, every ounce of 'want-to' you have in you—but it will be *worth it*. I can't promise you many things, Jena, but I *can* promise you that. It *will* be worth it."

"I do want to be normal." I sobbed. "I want a career and a family and a life, but it all feels so far away now. I'm light years away from what I was heading for, and I don't know how to find my way back. Even if I could, I'm so different now. I'm scarred."

Mark leaned back in his chair, spread his arms wide, and smiled. "Ah, but in love's service, only *wounded* soldiers can serve! Thank God for what He is bringing you through. You can't have a testimony without first having a test. You'll be stronger for it. You talk about being scarred. You know, Jena, scar tissue is actually *stronger* than normal healthy tissue. Your trials are reinforcing you."

"Yeah, well, then I'm gonna be one *tough* chick some day."

Mark folded his arms across his chest and smiled again. "You'd better believe it."

———

We had our work cut out for us. Mark's biblically balanced counsel combined with his firm authority made him a formidable opponent for my inner tormentor and its incessant, hissing voice. Several of our sessions were spiritual warfare at its most intense. It was a tumultuous time inside my head. My mind was a battlefield, and I had not yet decided which side would have my allegiance. In a flash of candor, I confessed to Mark one afternoon that I had planned my relapse before I'd ever entered treatment.

"Are you still planning to relapse after discharge?" he asked.

"Obviously, you want me to say no."

"Not if you'd be lying. I want your honesty. That's all I ever ask. You tell me you've planned your relapse since day one here, and I'm just curious if your plans have changed, or if there is any chance that they may change still."

"I'd like to think they've changed," I answered tentatively, "because otherwise I've just wasted tens of thousands of dollars. But if you're asking me to be completely honest, I don't know. I may get out of here and go home and find myself right back where I started."

"By chance or by choice? The motivation is key. If you go back to Illinois and surround yourself with the same things you were surrounded with before and you find yourself slipping into the old patterns of illness, that's scenario number one—

and there is a remedy for that. You change those surroundings or you make a conscious, intentional choice to respond to them in new ways. If you cannot respond to them in healthy ways, then you remove yourself from those surroundings until you feel you are better equipped. But if you are telling me you have already made the decision to return home and be a sick person for the rest of your life until you ultimately die, then no one can force any remedy upon you. It is entirely your choice to recover or not to recover. Do you want to die?"

"I have told you time and time again, I do not have a death wish. Why does nobody believe me?"

"I do believe you, Jena. I believe you have no death wish. So my question is, what's the payoff?"

"What do you mean?"

"What do you stand to gain by returning to your illness? There must be some potential payoff, or you wouldn't be considering it. How do you suppose remaining sick will serve you? What does disorder offer you that wellness doesn't?"

"I don't know."

"I think you do. By now you are beginning to understand what purpose your illness serves. Let me ask the question in reverse: What scares you about being healthy again?"

"I'm starting to look normal."

"And why is *normal* such a bad word? What does looking normal mean?"

"It means no one will know anything is wrong with me."

"Hmm." Mark paused a moment, considering, then asked, "Is there something wrong with you? What's wrong with you, Jena? What are the rest of us not seeing that you need us to see?"

I got up and walked to the window, peering out at the world outside. "I'm scared," I whispered.

"Of what?"

"Of living."

"And what is the scariest part about living? What part of life seems so daunting you cannot cope with it?"

"Failure. Disappointment. Loss, grief, embarrassment, shame, even fear itself." I was pacing, wringing my hands. "It's all just . . . too much. I need things to work out neatly, and they never do. I need to be perfect, or at least good enough, and I never will be. I cannot accept that—no matter what you or Deb or anyone else says or thinks."

"Why?"

"Because!" I leaned against the wall, my pulse throbbing in my ears.

"Because why?" Mark probed, matter-of-factly, as if he did not notice my emotional state at all. "Come on, Jena. You enjoy writing, right? So you are able to express yourself when you want to. So don't shut down on me now. What would be the scariest thing about showing the world that you are imperfect?"

I slid down the wall and pulled my knees to my chest. I let my head fall wearily to my knees and pleaded, "Do we have to talk about this?"

Mark turned his chair to face me in my new place on the floor behind him. "Oh, I think we do."

"I'm *tired*, Mark," I whimpered.

"I'll bet you are. I'd be tired, too, if I were always spinning my wheels trying to be perfect at everything."

"No, I'm tired of *this*. I'm tired of thinking about myself. It's been four months. I can't think about myself anymore."

Mark chuckled and scratched his forehead. "Well," he said, "I think we're trying to make up for lost time. You haven't given nearly enough thought to yourself for most of your life, so we have some catching up to do." He nudged my foot with his shoe. "And remember: thinking of yourself does not necessarily make you a selfish person."

I smirked. "What are you, a mind reader?"

"Apparently," Mark smiled, as he tapped his gray temple. "But the point is that you cannot bear the notion of being imperfect, and of revealing that imperfect soul to the world around you. I'm wondering what is so terrible about that idea."

I thought hard. I picked at the healing wound on my left hand, pressing until I felt the pain shoot up my arm, sending a chill through the top of my head. When I finally summoned the nerve to speak, I had nothing more than a whisper. "I don't want to let anybody down. I don't want to be a disappointment."

"A disappointment to whom? Besides yourself, I mean."

"God. My mom. My dad. My teachers and directors and professors and my *friends'* parents—just everyone."

"Because if you disappointed them . . . what? What would happen?"

"I would feel horrible. I would feel guilty."

"But you feel guilty *now*. Each time we meet we talk about how to help you get over these deep-seeded feelings of guilt and shame. So I would have to say your current system is not working. You feel guilty anyway."

I sighed deeply and closed my eyes. "I know."

Mark allowed me a few moments of silence. Then he set his notebook and pen down on the floor and reclined in his chair, putting his feet up on the table in front of him. "You want to know what I think? I think the reason God doesn't allow any one of us to achieve perfection is because perfect people would be *boring.* Think about it. Some of the greatest figures in the Bible were real knuckleheads. David was guilty of adultery and murder. Peter had such a hot temper that he whacked off a guy's ear pretty much on a whim. Timothy had a great call to ministry on his life, but his nerves were so shot that Paul had to tell him to drink some wine to calm his stomach. Poor kid probably had ulcers. These were not perfect people, by any stretch, and look at how God used them for His glory. Don't you think maybe—just maybe—God doesn't expect you to be perfect, either?"

"Maybe," I whispered, staring at the floor.

Mark leaned in again and matched my quiet tone. "Can I let you in on a secret? When you mess up and fall short of perfection, God is not shocked. It doesn't catch Him by surprise. When your heavenly Father looks at you, guess what He sees? He sees Jesus. Your imperfections are covered by the blood of Christ, kid."

I started to cry again. Mark's words of truth warmed me and soothed my pain like a balm of healing. I desperately wanted him to keep talking.

"Don't you know you're the apple of God's eye? Jena, God doesn't look at you and see flaws. He doesn't see a list of sins and shortcomings. He's not looking at the labels you've let people stick on you, or even the ones you've stuck on yourself. They mean nothing to Him, and they can never change His opinion of you. His opinion is that you are unspeakably special; you've been set apart for His glory. Do you know what that means? Jena, He *chose* you. You! He didn't choose you and say, 'Well, I hope she doesn't screw up' or 'Well, here goes nothing.' No! God chose you, knowing the end from the beginning. He knew you'd be sitting here today with me. He knew you would have struggles—in fact, Jesus promised all of us that we would have trouble in this life, didn't He? I cannot stress this to you enough, my friend: *God is not mad at you.*"

"Even when everyone else seems to be?"

"Right. And if everyone in your family or everyone in the world is mad at you, but God isn't, guess what? God wins. He's still the majority. If God is for us, who can be against us? And," Mark said, rising from his chair to signal the end of our session, "if God's not mad at you, here's a novel thought: maybe *you* don't need to be mad at *yourself* anymore."

The Agony of Victory

t is dinnertime in the main lodge. I sit down and survey my tray's contents. Something is wrong. There seems to be less food than usual. I squint at my meal card, reading the checkmarks under the dietary exchanges. "2 proteins, 2 starches, 1 fat, 1 vegetable, 1 fruit." It *is* less food. I panic. They must have allowed me to get too fat. I tried to tell them I was gaining too much!

My heart races. My palms sweat, despite the chilly air in the dining room. I try to calm myself, take a deep breath, and bring my meal card with me to the end of the table where Carol the nurse is sitting.

"Um, Carol?" I whisper.

"Yes, dear?"

"Um, hi."

She laughs, a smallish, bemused laugh. "Hi yourself."

"Yeah, so I noticed my exchanges are down, and I just wondered if you could tell me why. I mean, I'm glad and all—this is what I've been asking for all along—but I just wondered if you knew . . ."

Carol pushes up her reading glasses and peers over my card. She smiles kindly. "You've been put on maintenance, hon."

My eye twitches. I clear my throat. My voice is froggy. "Maintenance?"

"Yes. You're no longer on a gaining plan. These are your exchanges for weight maintenance. This is the plan you will stay on from now on."

I feel lightheaded. There is a tight rubber band squeezing my ribcage, and breathing is difficult. There are buzzing voices in the room, in my head. Carol gently takes my hand. "Congratulations, Jena," she says discreetly, as if this is a good thing. "You've met your goal."

I snatch my hand out of hers, as if the contact stings. My chin trembles. I bolt out of the room.

Eventually, I collect myself (though the tears refuse to dam) and Carol convinces me to return to the table. I push my plate away. I sit with my head buried in the crook of my elbow. I silently sob through the meal, begging God to forgive me for hating His creation—myself—so violently in that moment.

———

"I wish someone would have told me ahead of time," I complained to Mark that afternoon, nervously twisting my hair in my fingers. "I wish I could have had a few weeks to prepare myself for what was coming."

"And what would you have done to make yourself feel better prepared to deal with this news?"

"I don't know," I said, biting at my cuticles. "I would have read more affirmations or started praying for God to give me peace or something."

"Can't you do those things now? Is there a significant window of opportunity for seeking peace from God?"

"No." I rolled my eyes, still biting away.

"I must say, Jena, you certainly seem more agitated than usual," Mark observed. "What is causing you to feel so uneasy?"

"Well, *duhhh*, Mark," I said, shooting him a look.

"Okay, don't take my head off!" Mark laughed. "Are you telling me that was a dumb question?"

I pulled my finger out of my mouth and crossed my arms over my chest. "Do *you* think it was a dumb question?"

"You're more sarcastic than usual today," Mark observed with a bemused smile. "Where do you suppose the sarcasm is coming from?"

"Where do *you* think it's coming from?"

"Ahhh," Mark said, reclining in his leather chair. "I see what we're doing here. Today you get to ask the questions. You get to be the therapist."

"Do you have a problem with that?" I countered, half enjoying the exchange and half annoyed.

"There you go again," Mark said, pointing his finger playfully. "Well, if you're the therapist now, you must not be needing any further care, so I should recommend you for discharge."

"Might as well," I said, shaking my leg as fast as it would move. Nervous leg shaking burns calories—and becomes a terrible habit common among anoretics.

Mark looked at me quizzically. "Wow," he said slowly. "You are *really* ticked off, aren't you?"

"Yes!" I yelled.

"Why?" he whispered.

"Because I'm . . ."

"You're what?"

"I'm . . ."

"Say it."

I squeezed my eyes closed as bitter tears ran down my cheeks. "No."

"It isn't true, Jena. You're not what you fear you've become. And I think you know that becoming fat is not your real fear."

"Yes, it *is*!" I shot back, almost screaming.

"No, it isn't," Mark said nonchalantly, as if he knew everything.

"It's been my fear for as long as I can remember, and thanks to the *stupid nutritionist*, it's gonna take me forever t—" I stopped myself and stared at the ceiling. "Forget it."

"To starve yourself back to death's door after I release you? Still planning to relapse, huh?" Mark asked casually.

"It doesn't matter. Nothing matters."

"Because you're no longer underweight? Is that why nothing matters?"

I sat silently, screaming on the inside, wanting to unzip my fat suit and crawl out.

"Jena," Mark said. "You are more than your body."

"Oh, spare me, Mark," I said, rolling my eyes. "The fortune-cookie language is *not* gonna help today."

"No, spare *me,* Jena," Mark retorted. "Spare me the sarcasm, just for a second. Just long enough to get real and get back to the basics. You need a refresher course on the basics. I'll say it again: *you* are *more* than your body."

I said nothing.

Mark continued, "You could get in a car accident tomorrow and be disfigured, and you would still be you. The external is not all that there is to you. If you believe your Bible, one day your body is gonna just return to dust anyway, and we'll get new bodies in heaven. Is there some reason you are in such a hurry to return to dust? Is there some logical explanation for why you're in such a rush to die?"

"Come on, Mark, I'm *not!* Enough with the suicide stuff. I'm *not* suicidal!"

"This is old news, Jena. There's quick suicide, and there's slow suicide. You've chosen the slow way to kill yourself, and you get to take others with you for the ride. They get to *watch* you wither and die. What do you want people to think while they watch you die?"

"I don't care what other people think," I said, pouting.

"Baloney. You care what I think," Mark said. "If you didn't, it wouldn't bother you that I think you're trying to die."

"But it's not true."

"So it bothers you that I believe something about you that is untrue? But *you* believe lots of things about yourself that are untrue. Don't you?" He continued, "You believe you are fat, and that bothers me. More importantly, you believe you are unworthy of God's goodness, unworthy of all the good things He has provided for us in this life. You believe you are awkward and inadequate and stupid, when you are quite the opposite on all counts. You believe lies, Jena. You've made quite a life-long habit of believing lies. Doesn't that bother you? Aren't you ready to stop being fooled?"

I pulled my knees to my chest and covered them with my sweatshirt. "I wish I could."

"You can, Jena!" Mark asserted. "All the things I have because of Jesus, you can have, too. You can have peace—with others, with yourself, with God. You can have joy—without feeling guilty for experiencing pleasure."

"I don't—"

"I know," Mark interrupted me. "You don't deserve pleasure. Whatever. If you really want to split hairs, you don't deserve anything at all. Neither do I. We're sinners, we've fallen short of God's holy standards, and we deserve no good thing on this earth. I can agree with you on that much. But that's why Jesus came! He was the only perfect person—ever—and He lets us ride in on His coattails, so to speak. That's grace. Grace is getting good things we don't deserve. And mercy is *not* getting all the bad things we *do* deserve. Can you agree with me on that?"

I nodded, wiping my eyes with my sleeves.

"Okay," Mark went on, "then let me ask you this. When you give someone a gift and he refuses it, how does that feel? Kind of insulting, right? Or at least disappointing?"

"Yeah."

"Sure it is—even if the gift didn't cost you much. But this gift that Jesus wants you to have—this free gift of life, and all the good things the redeemed life has to offer—cost Him everything. *Everything,* Jena. It costs His *life.* It cost His precious blood—*innocent* blood. That's how much He loves you and how desperately He wants you to have this gift. And yet here you sit, ticked off because you've gotten a tiny bit closer to living. It seems a little absurd, really."

"But if God wants me to enjoy peace or life to the full, or whatever, then He doesn't want me to hate myself. And being at this weight—whatever it is, since it's some huge government secret or something—makes me hate myself. How is that supposed to help me enjoy life and live for Jesus? Tell me that."

"Well," Mark sighed, "you're gonna have to let go. You can't be the one in control anymore."

"Oh, okay," I said, heavy on the sarcasm.

"Why do you suppose it's so important to you to be in control?" Mark asked, putting his feet up on the coffee table.

"Because otherwise everything falls apart."

"What's everything?"

"Like . . . I don't know, just everything. Plans for the future. Relationships. Someone has to be in control to keep the peace."

"And that has to be you because other people are dropping the ball? Or because you're the best person for the job?"

"I don't know," I said. "I don't want to incriminate anyone, if that's what you're trying to make me do."

"No, no, no," Mark said. "We're not out to get anybody. Who are you worried about incriminating, anyway?"

"My parents. Everyone is always trying to blame this stuff on my parents, and I don't think that's fair because they've done the best they could. They weren't perfect, but no one is perfect."

"That's true," Mark said. "But even good parents make mistakes. Even good parents can cause real damage to their children. Denying that damage is not going to help anyone, least of all you."

"I don't want you to think bad things about my mom and dad," I said.

"So you do care what people think." Mark smiled.

"Shut up," I said, cracking a slight smile myself.

"Well, that's significant, actually," he said. "If it's important to you that others not think ill of your folks, you've probably spent a lot of time keeping secrets. Just about every family has them, not just yours. I imagine you've spent a great deal of time and energy trying to cover the sins of others, and you can't do that."

"But that's what we're supposed to do as Christians," I said, truly confused. "Aren't we supposed to turn the other cheek when we're wronged? And doesn't Scripture say that love covers a multitude of sins?"

"Are you Jesus, Jena?"

"No."

"Okay. Then why are you expecting yourself to atone for other people's mistakes? You can't do it. And as for turning the other cheek, yes, we are called to forgive others. But we are never called to deny we were ever hurt. You can't forgive what you deny, because if it never happened, there is nothing to forgive. Right?"

"I guess . . ."

"Okay. So you have to recognize what happened, call it what

it is—if it's sin, it's sin—and then you can begin the work of forgiveness. And that is where real healing begins."

"That sounds . . . hard," I said.

"It's incredibly hard!" Mark laughed. "And it hurts like crazy at times. But forgiving others isn't only about letting them off the hook. It's also about letting ourselves off the hook. It sets us free from having to manage the facade and keep secrets and be the chief peacekeeper. It takes those who've wronged us off of our hook, so to speak, and puts them on God's hook, where they belong. Let God deal with them. Forgiveness isn't about denial; it's about reassigning judgment. Let God be their judge, so you don't have to be. It's too much for you to be the defense attorney for all of the people you love. You don't have to defend them; you just have to love them."

"Hmm," I said after a moment. "I like that."

"Doesn't that feel better? Doesn't that sound like a load off? It takes some real weight off of us when we can do that," Mark said, winking at me. "Pardon the pun."

As autumn blew in, the time came to say good-bye to Mark and move to Remuda's transitional living program in Chandler, Arizona. October was a weird month. We all seemed a bit "itchy" and suddenly claustrophobic and crowded within the Remuda campus. We became crabby and impatient and mouthy. October signaled the beginning of that three-month block of holidays—Halloween, Thanksgiving, and Christmas— that only reminded us all how homesick we were.

Nina left treatment in October, against medical advice. Tiff buckled down and made amazing progress in her recovery work, earning level four status and often leaving to go and work out in a nearby gym, where she would later take a job as a personal trainer. Andrea, still having never uttered another word in the four months I had known her, was released a few weeks before I was, though she still appeared strangely frail despite her weight restoration. She left a tiny folded note on my breakfast tray the morning she departed. It read:

Jena,
Thank you for being my friend here. I know I never did anything to let you know that I appreciated it, but I did. All those times when you sat with me and talked and talked and talked some

more ☺, *I really was listening, and I liked spending time with*
you. You made me feel less alone here, and I am going to miss
you when we both go home.
    Love you, girl!
    Andrea H.

I read that letter over and over, marveling at the tiny,
perfect purple letters. I felt I had just been given the world's
most prestigious award.

———

A few weeks later, it was my turn to leave for Chandler. As
the shuttle van pulled away from the Ranch, I cried, watching it
grow smaller in the distance—the horses, the adobe buildings,
the palm trees, the people—some I had come to love and
would miss, some I was secretly thankful to bid adieu.

As I left the structure of intensive inpatient care at the
Ranch and prepared to transition into Remuda's more flexible
residential program, part of me wanted to embrace this next
phase of treatment, and yet another part relished the safety of
Remuda Ranch and its palpable sense of the closeness of God.
In one sense I longed to run full-speed back into the black cave
of sickness that had once brought me such solace. I missed
my frailty, my naked bones, the feeling of shrinking away from
the world. Anorexia seemed familiar and welcoming. I did not
remember the starving years as they truly had been; I did not
remember the paralyzing fear of food, the horrible paranoia,
the sleepless nights and weeks and months, the strange phobias
that kept me always looking over my shoulder, wary of the
world and its inhabitants. I remembered only the excitement of
feeling myself get smaller and smaller and smaller still with each
passing day. I wanted that excitement to suck me up again.

The van pulled into a short cul-de-sac bordered by a handful of cookie-cutter southwestern-style homes with clay tile roofs and well-manicured desert landscaping. "All righty, girls," the driver said. "Here we are. Welcome to Chandler."

We yawned and stretched, saying little as we took in our new surroundings. At intake sessions, we signed forms and got weighed and were examined and interviewed and welcomed. Then we were led to the houses we had been assigned. Each home housed five or six girls—some from inpatient treatment at the Ranch, some coming directly to Chandler from other programs or from the outside world.

I was assigned to a house at the back of the cul-de-sac, a ranch-style home with three bedrooms and a quaint backyard bordered by a peach-colored stucco wall. I entered through the front door and called out, "Hello? Anybody home?"

"Hello!" sang out a friendly voice from the back of the house. And then she came into view—Ellen, the angry girl I had known at the Ranch who had pushed the pregnant MHT. We ran to one another and embraced. A wave of fear swept over me, though, as I realized she was no longer as thin as she had been when she left the Ranch. I was terrified I would gain even more weight in residential care, and I had an urgent desire to run away, then and there.

"We're gonna be roomies," Ellen squealed. "Yay!"

"Yay!" I echoed.

"Come on, I'll show you our room; we're lucky we get the one closest to the bathroom."

I laughed as I followed her down the peach-carpeted hall to our small bedroom on the other side of the house.

"Voilà," Ellen said, "the nest."

"Cool," I said, trying to contain my ambivalence.

She helped me unpack, hang my posters and cards on the wall with blue sticky putty, stack my stuffed animals in a pyramid on my twin bed. She filled me in on who had come and gone, who had called from home, who was doing well, who had already relapsed, and about herself.

"I have come so far, Jena, I swear. I'm more peaceful now. I'm working through all that anger I had for years. I just want to live now. I don't want to starve anymore; I don't ever want to go back to that place in my life, not for anything. You know."

"Mmm," I said, wishing I could agree more enthusiastically. I was still gripped by an incredible irrational fear of getting fat. I was nowhere near the freedom Ellen had embraced. I had a sense that I just needed to put in my time for another couple of months, and then I could go home and lose whatever weight had been put on me. *I'm sorry, God,* I said. *Forgive me.*

"Hello? Hello?" a quiet voice called from the front hall.

"We're back here," Ellen called back. She turned to me. "Do you have any idea who that is?"

"Should I?"

"Just wait," she whispered, holding up her finger and focusing expectantly toward the hall.

Suddenly a shadow fell across the peach carpet in front of where we sat on the floor. "Hi, Jena."

I looked up and nearly screamed for joy. "Andrea!" I said, jumping up to hug her. "You're talking!" She laughed as I squeezed her tightly. "I'm sorry," I said. "I've just . . . I've never heard you speak! This is so exciting!"

She laughed shyly and glanced at Ellen. I got the feeling Andrea was still a girl of few words, but to hear her speak even just those few words was amazing, like hearing a toddler speak for the very first time.

"How are you?" I asked Andrea, still holding her tightly by the shoulders.

"Good," she smiled. "I'm doing . . . well." She looked almost embarrassed by this assertion, as if the state of being "well" were something secret and playfully naughty.

"That's great!" I said, still taking in the sight of her. Her formerly blue translucent skin seemed to have grown more milky white and opaque, and her face had a touch of color. She was wearing lip gloss and had pulled her wild hair into a ponytail. She still held her head at a slight downward angle, as if shielding her face from the sun, but she looked me in the eye. Her voice was the loveliest sound I had heard in months.

"Well," she said, her lips curving slightly as though hiding a mischievous secret, "I just wanted to say hi." She moved away, still awkward and slow, like an old lady after major surgery. Ellen and I watched out the window as Andrea walked in slow motion down the street to her house.

"Wow," I said. "Miracles still happen."

Ellen smiled, still watching Andrea. "If we let them."

———

I would stay at Chandler for nearly three months, from the beginning of October until my birthday on Christmas Eve, which was the date I was officially discharged. I remember this time fondly, with images of laughing girls and magazine collages and autumn air and field trips.

There were five of us in the house, a nice mixture of ages and personalities, all of us a little crazy: a human fruit salad. There was Ellen—type triple A personality, extremely intelligent, emotionally wounded, and a fun partner in rebellion. There was Meghan—bulimic, admitted directly to Chandler without a previous stay at the Ranch, hyper, obsessive, bipolar, and indescribably gorgeous with her naturally spiraled long honey blonde hair and almond-shaped blue eyes. There was Kimmy, who had been at the Ranch with me, but whom I had not gotten to know previously—tall, blond, athletic, dual diagnosis of compulsive exerciser and orthorexia, which is an obsession with healthy and organic eating coupled with a fear of food that is perceived as impure. Jackie, who was also a direct-to-Chandler admit, was in her midforties and an amazingly gifted gospel singer with a palpable passion for God, a compulsive overeater, and the self-appointed "mother" of the house. And there was me.

Chandler, now called the Remuda Life Program, was far less structured than the inpatient program at the Ranch. Like any halfway house, it was designed to help patients transition back into the real world. The daily schedule included one-on-one therapy, art and other "expressive" therapies, process group, and chapel. There were also frequent field trips, with the Remuda van stuffed full of girls laughing and singing to the radio and doing our best to drive the MHTs crazy with unruly behavior, loudness, and pent-up energy that burst forth when we were "let out."

Most of these trips were casual and recreational. There would be quick trips to Walmart to blow money sent from family back home, and where someone always seemed to get caught trying to stock up on laxatives or artificial sweetener. We enjoyed a carefree excursion to a fall festival in town, where we all bounced gleefully like children inside a giant inflatable pumpkin, and where Ellen and I sneaked off to a concession stand for a taboo Diet Coke, which we guzzled much too quickly while looking over our shoulders as though we were shooting heroin in the middle of the town square. We went to the library to check out books to read during free time; most of us huddled in the magazine section, surreptitiously poring over the glossy pages full of stick-thin celebrities, punishing ourselves as we compared our "healthy" bodies to theirs.

Always, in these rebellious moments, someone would step in and be the voice of reason. Usually it was Jackie, who was everyone's mama. "Y'all quit that now!" she'd say, lowering her brows in disapproval. "Jesus tryin' to set y'all free, and y'all's just fightin' Him every chance y'all get!" This was my personal favorite Jackie rebuke: "Y'all bein' stupid, and Jackie ain't got no patience for stupid!" She would walk away, shaking her head, beaded braids click-clacking as she muttered at us under her breath. I absolutely adored her.

Being around Jackie was humbling for me. Her eating disorder was a threat to her health in ways opposite to mine. She became obese at an early age. She therefore thought it was ridiculous for those of us who were relatively thin to despair of our figures, demanding our bodies succumb to unrealistic standards of perfection.

Overhearing a conversation Kimmy and I were having on the back patio regarding our muscular calves, which we referred to as "mannish," Jackie slid open the sliding screen door and said, "Y'all make me crazy, you know that? God gave you perfectly good legs to get around on, but noooo, they ain't good enough for you. Y'all oughtta be ashamed of yourselves! If'n I was you, I'd get to repentin', right quick!" Then she stomped back to stirring her pot of chili on the stove, singing "How Great Thou Art" at a glorious, unashamed volume.

Kimmy and I looked at one another and saw the conviction in one another's eyes. We laughed to keep from crying, and we apologized to Jackie over dinner that night, told her she was absolutely right, and thanked her for setting us straight. Honestly, I often wish Jackie lived with me today.

Nina came to visit me at Chandler in November. She had taken a two-week vacation with her husband, Eric; by the time they visited me, she was noticeably thinner. I worried, I warned, I threatened.

I envied.

It was a Friday night, so I got a three-hour pass. Nina and I drove around town in her rental car, singing with the radio and letting the wind tousle our hair through the moon roof. We spoke of the future and God and music and movies and books. We talked about mutual friends and friends back home. We did not talk about her dramatic weight loss, my sick jealousy, our fears for each other's well-being. Not at first.

We ate at a Marie Callender's restaurant in Chandler, putting on a little show for each other, following our exchanges, practicing our new life skills. Nina ordered a veggie burger, I ordered a grilled vegetable platter. Neither of us mentioned we had ordered food that we perceived as "safe," which is considered disordered behavior. We shared an unspoken agreement that we were out to enjoy each other's company, and we would not let anything get in the way—anything like honesty, for example.

After hanging out in a bookstore poring over titles in the Addiction & Recovery aisle, we rode around with the windows open and listened to the Sarah McLachlan CD Nina had bought. The scene became poignant as we began singing along: *I will remember you / Will you remember me? / Don't let your life pass you by / Weep not for the memories.* We both started to cry, and Nina had to pull over. She grabbed my hand, squeezing tightly as she waited to be able to speak. Her hand felt bony and cold, like that of a corpse.

"Nina," I said, breaking the tearful silence, "I don't want to lose you."

"I know," she said, in a shaky, broken whisper, as her tears spotted the fabric of her khaki shorts.

"I don't want this to be the last time I see you, Nin," I said, attempting to meet her eyes for emphasis. "Do you understand me?"

Nina dabbed at her eyes and tossed her head back, staring up through the roof at huge stars in the Arizona sky. "I know. I know, I know."

I was quiet a moment, not wanting to say too much. "I'm worried about you."

Nina's blue eyes shone with tears waiting to fall. "I'm worried about you, too!"

"I'm doing well, though," I said. "I'm fine. You can see that. But it's only been two weeks, and already you do not look well. I know you don't want to hear this, but you look sick again. And that really scares me."

Nina turned her face away and began crying again.

"I don't want to lose you," I repeated.

Nina nodded and squeezed my hand, harder still.

Staff began giving me more and more rope, granting me passes and allowing visitors. Mom flew in for a week in November, and we had a blast getting lost on sightseeing expeditions. It was difficult to see her again—or rather, to be seen by her—since when she had left after Family Week, I had still been significantly underweight. She gushed about how great I looked at my healthy body weight, and I bit my tongue to keep from telling her how desperately I wanted to lose twenty pounds once I got back home.

Dad came to visit for an evening as well, which meant the world to me. I felt a new closeness to him since our moment of truth at the Ranch, and although we never spoke of it again, it seemed that moment had smoothed away years of wrinkles in our relationship. We went out to dinner, and he told me I looked beautiful. He asked what I planned to do with my future, and I told him I might study art therapy so I could help others.

Hollow

I began to push fairly hard for a December release, in order to be home for my birthday on Christmas Eve. I looked around at cacti decorated with Christmas lights and decided there was simply no place like home for the holidays. Besides, I had maintained my weight, I was eating on my own, and there seemed little more I could take away from the program. It was time to move on.

"Can you commit to staying healthy at home?" asked Donna, my therapist at Chandler. "Do you really feel moving back home is the best thing for you?"

"I don't know," I said. "But I can't afford to stay out here, so going back home is my only choice."

"Will you commit to attending weekly meetings and finding another counselor back in Illinois?" Donna asked, as if she knew the answer.

"Of course, Donna. You have nothing to worry about," I replied, winking. "Unless, of course, you don't release me for my birthday."

Patient granted release for 12/23/96. Recommend aggressive relapse-prevention measures be taken. Elevated mood; perhaps has unrealistic expectations of herself as she leaves treatment. Body image continues to need improvement; little progress made. Meal plan upon release: 1700 c. daily. Ht 66", Wt 128.

It was late morning once I had checked my many bags at the Phoenix airport and found a spot to camp out while I awaited my flight back home to Chicago. I planned to spend time praying and journaling, processing my mixture of emotions like a good little patient fresh out of treatment. As soon as I opened my journal and uncapped my pen, I was distracted in a most inconvenient way.

A girl about my age walked past—a painfully thin girl, looking terribly lost—trailing an overstuffed duffel bag. She wore black leggings and gray Birkenstock sandals on her bony blue feet, and had a big red sweatshirt tied around her tiny waist. In her short-sleeved T-shirt, her sticklike arms were proudly displayed, swinging back and forth as she propelled herself forward, eyes alight with confusion and panic. The skin beneath her eyes was steely gray with traces of purple, broken blood vessels. I knew I should help her, but I debated as I stared. *Do I tell her I just came from the place where she's going? I'm fifty pounds heavier than she is; will I scare her in the other direction?* I felt my opportunity slip away as she walked on, and suddenly words leapt from my mouth.

"Are you lost?"

"Oh, yes, yes," she said, in a Polish accent. "You know where—emm, where coffee restaurant is here?"

"Oh," I said, "are you looking for the café?"

"Yes, yes, café," she said. "I am supposed to meet—emm, someone is picking me. They are picking me and I am lost!" She began to laugh at herself, shaking her head, her thin white-blonde chin-length hair swinging.

"I know where it is," I said, looking for a familiar sign. "It's way on the other end of this floor. I can help you find it."

"Oh," she said. "Yes, yes. Thank you. I am afraid they will miss me."

"Your friends?" I asked, fishing for confirmation of my suspicions. I stuffed my journal into my bag and slung it over my shoulder as we began to walk.

"Emm, no," she said. "I am going—they are picking me to take me to—a place."

She wore a beaded cross around her neck, which she held with her left hand as we walked. I had enough clues, and I took a risk. "Are you going to Remuda?"

She turned, her light blue eyes wide and bloodshot. "Yes! That is the place I am going!"

I smiled. "That's where I'm coming from."

She pointed at me. "You?"

She thinks you're fat, you know, the voice said. *You should have never told her. Have you forgotten what you look like now, you soft gluttonous pig?*

"Yep," I answered. "I was there since last July. How long are you supposed to stay?"

"It is trial," she said. "Not long, I hope!" She laughed as we caught sight of the café sign in the distance. "Okay, I see. I can go from here."

"Okay," I said, as we stopped. "Well . . . good luck to you." Somehow it didn't seem like the right thing to say. I tried again. "Hey . . . what's your name?"

"Katya," she said, shaking my hand so briskly I thought it would come off my arm. "I am Katya."

"I'm Jena," I said. "I'm going to be praying for you, Katya. Remuda is a good place." I placed my other hand on top of hers. "It changed my life."

"Thank you, thank you," Katya said, pulling me into a hug, her movements brisk and sharp and tense, her bony clavicle biting into my chest. "I will say prayers, too. Thank you!" She took off for the Patient Transporter from Remuda waiting for her. Suddenly, she spun on her heel. "Jena," she called out to me, "stay well!"

I smiled, relieved I hadn't scared her. The voice argued, *She doesn't want to stay long because she doesn't want to leave there looking like you.* I waved and nodded to Katya and watched over my shoulder as she greeted the transporter. She stood there, so pitifully birdlike and frail that her feet looked out of proportion with her spindly calves. Watching her, I remembered how terrified I was when I arrived in this same airport, not knowing what awaited me. I felt a wave of pity for her wash over me, and I thanked God for carrying me through the past seven months.

Then, of course, I felt a bigger wave—more like a tsunami —of jealousy come over me, nearly taking me down. To this day, if I were to see someone on the street as thin as Katya, I would experience the same reaction, and to this day, I cannot explain why. I do not think such extreme thinness is attractive. I am angered by the skeletal standards of beauty by which our fashion industry is governed. I feel quite passionate about fostering a healthy sense of self and body image in impressionable girls, several of whom I keep close in my own life for that very purpose. These things notwithstanding, the jealousy still comes, still stings, still momentarily breathes fire-blasts of shame in my face.

This double-mindedness frustrates me. I am a committed Christian, and by doctrine I support life and life "to the full" (according to John 10:10). Nothing is more fully in direct opposition to life than an eating disorder. An eating disorder steals life, whether the sufferer lives or dies. It sucks the joy out of life and renders a person void of vitality, spontaneity, gaiety, and freedom. An eating disorder is an invisible cage, a punishment I would not wish on my worst enemy.

A few weeks after I flew home, I found out from a friend at the Ranch that Katya had stayed less than a week before leaving AMA (against medical advice). Only God knows if she is alive today. I suspect she may have been double-minded as well, both wanting to remain haunted and longing to break free from the ghosts. Sometimes the right choice is just too scary to make. Ultimately, though, even the double-minded must choose.

As I waited to board the plane that would fly me back to the place where *my* journey had begun, I knew I had a choice to make. It was the same choice I had been faced with all along, the same choice that was before me even prior to spending seven months in inpatient treatment. It was a simple choice, really—like a multiple-choice quiz with only two possible answers, allowing a fifty-fifty chance to pass.

One question. Life or death?

CHAPTER 24

I touched down in Chicago on December 23, 1996, the day before my birthday. My mom and her boyfriend, Dennis, picked me up at O'Hare, and Mom and I were simply giddy. I was overjoyed to be home, and it was Christmastime. I loved that there was snow covering the ground and frosting the treetops and not a cactus in sight. There was only one teeny problem: I weighed 128 pounds, more than forty pounds more than the last time I'd been home.

The three of us went to a Cracker Barrel somewhere along I-55 for dinner. I was extremely uneasy, both because I was being watched by the food police and because Dennis kept looking me with a wide grin he could not seem to contain.

"What?" I asked him across the table, my fork poised above my chef salad. *"What?"*

"Nothing," he smiled, still watching me. "I'm just lookin' at you, that's all."

I tried not to be self-conscious. Years later, Dennis finally told me he had simply not been able to take his eyes off of me that night because, as he said, "You were glowing."

I doubt I was actually backlit in any way. Mom and Dennis had been used to seeing me with gray skin and dark under-eye circles for so long I must have appeared in technicolor by comparison. It never occurred to me Dennis might stare at me because I looked *good*. In my imagination, he was laughing at how fat I had become.

Pig face, the voice hissed quietly, as if she were speaking underwater. *Don't look down; they'll see your double chin.* I hadn't heard from my evil twin in a while, and now that I was back on my own, she seemed aware that it was her cue to take the stage again. *Tomorrow, we cut back. It won't take long this time. We'll get your bones back, honey.*

As homesick as I had become in seven months in Arizona, I soon knew that coming home to Illinois had thrust me directly back into the danger zone. Friends who had written to me at the Ranch so faithfully for all those months were relieved to have me back and expected me to be "all better now." But I was only partly better. My body had healed, my weight had been restored, my face had filled out and gotten its color back. This seemed a cruel joke: I looked well on the outside but was as sick as ever inside my head. It was like bleeding from a wound no one else could see.

I had learned some powerful things in treatment, had been given powerful tools to employ in my fight. Most importantly, I had embarked on a real relationship with my God, when before I had known Him mostly in a religious, nominal sense. All of these good things, in fact, saved my life. But not right away. Not dramatically, and not overnight, which was what my friends and family had hoped. The seeds had been planted at Remuda, but their fruits would reveal themselves in time. First, the weeds would grow back.

The team at Remuda had warned us that relapse is most likely to occur soon following release from the program, and that this would be the time to be especially diligent and intentional about protecting ourselves from people and situations that triggered disordered responses. So, I reasoned, it shouldn't have come to anyone's surprise when I began losing weight.

For the first several weeks, I truly did attempt to follow my assigned dietary plan. I measured portions and counted exchanges and drank milk and took meds. I followed the plan more out of habit than out of any real desire to stay healthy. But habits, whether good or bad, can be broken.

First, snacks fell by the wayside. Easy to reason: not everyone snacks between meals. Life is busy; we can't always be bothered. Then breakfast shrank to a piece of fruit and black coffee. Then lunch—so frivolous, so inconvenient, right there in the middle of the day—was eliminated. Lots of professionals work through their lunch hours, I reasoned. This was normal. Dinner, of course, was harder to escape. I usually ate this meal with Mom, whose worried eyes convicted me.

The weight began to fall off. I began again to look a little haunted, a little gray. I started getting cold again around the beginning of February when my period again stopped. Friends grew oddly silent in my presence, as though I ruined the party simply by entering the room.

I had been given tools at Remuda that could surely have enabled me to walk in recovery and health. Jesus had made the way for me. It wasn't that my healing "didn't take"; I simply didn't feel ready to *take* His *healing*. People question how some of us can be Christ-followers and yet struggle with a psychological illness. I usually answer that it certainly isn't Jesus' fault.

There were a few elements at play in my post-treatment relapse. Certainly I was prideful. On one level, I didn't want those around me who were pulling for my recovery to have the satisfaction of knowing—and seeing for themselves—that I had "given in" and regained weight.

Not only was I struggling with pride, I was still deceived in many ways. I still believed that extreme thinness—if I could *just* get back there—was going to bring me the peace and relief I sought. This was a lie of epic proportions, and I—fresh out of treatment, healed in body while still sick in the head—bought it.

I was prideful, I was deceived, and I was scared. I had spent almost a year in treatment, and I had left with a weight of debt and saw no possibility of returning to college. I had no job. I was twenty years old and saw no way out of my mother's home, and the very thing that had become my identity—sickness—had been covered over by forty pounds of flesh. So with pride, deception, and fear at the helm of my ship, I sank. Quickly.

———

My mother's home soon became a revolving door for my friends from treatment, and I am grateful she was so willing to open her doors to these dear women I had befriended. She may have been desperate to keep me surrounded by others who understood my struggle, as Mom herself must have felt truly alienated by its complexities. She said very little but watched me with no small amount of concern and frustration as I shrank in the months following my release from Remuda. Perhaps she hoped that inviting my fellow eating disorder warriors into the house would encourage me to get back in line.

In the spring, Nina flew in smelling like soap and looking like death. I had missed her terribly since we had last seen each other at Chandler, when it had been apparent she was inching her way back down the slippery slope. Both of us had been eagerly looking forward to our reunion, and I harbored shiny fantasies of what the visit would be like—hugs and giggles and movies and board games and sisterly bonding, singing along to uplifting Christian music as we painted our toenails and styled each other's hair, smiling in the mirror. It would be lovely, and we would be the same "us" we had been at the Ranch, but now we would be free from the watchful eyes of staff, free to go places and do things and drink coffee together whenever we pleased.

It was different. It was still special and sentimental because it was a reunion and reunions are special and sentimental, but it was not as I had imagined. We ourselves were not as I had imagined. We were not the same "us" we had been. We were sick. We were compromised and weakened. We put on our best faces for each other, spritzed ourselves with perfume and smiled brightly and laughed as heartily as we could, but we were only masquerading. We were empty shells of the people we had been at the Ranch and each was hoping the other would not notice.

We noticed.

Hugging Nina then was like hugging a lampshade or a birdcage, and eating with her was like dining with a skeleton at the head of the table, whom no one was supposed to acknowledge. I imagine her experience of hugging and eating with me was the same. The two of us must have been utterly ridiculous to behold.

We did not speak of it. We pretended, and we let each other pretend. We made believe we were eating well and looking as healthy as ever. We went to church together, sang songs of worship to the God who so persistently and patiently knocked at the doors of our hearts, and we talked about our love for Him, our longing to grow closer to Him, our desire to follow His plan and purpose for our lives. We did not, however, mention that His plan and purpose might include a mandate to end the slow suicide we had resumed.

As Nina and I hugged our good-byes at the airport the

day she left to go back to Boston, we were both aware of the possibility that one or both of us could very well die before we would see each other again. It was a long and tearful hug.

But because God is good and has a mighty, restraining hand that often shields us from the dangers we deserve, Nina's frail body held out and I received a card from her six months later, with a long letter scrawled in her unique tiny handwriting. Inside were two photos of Nina wearing a cropped athletic tank top and black spandex yoga pants. She is terribly thin, all bony twig legs and spindly arms, like Olive Oyl ready for a workout. And she is six months pregnant. I stared in disbelief; she looked like a Biafra child who had swallowed a volleyball.

A long telephone conversation followed, and Nina told me that just when she was ready to give up on recovery and had begun entertaining thoughts of suicide, she had learned about the baby. The baby was a medical miracle, given Nina's physical state at the time of conception. The baby would be a girl named Hannah, one of the most beautiful children I have ever seen. She would change Nina's life forever.

Motherhood gave my friend someone to care for and nurture and love, and it took her mind off of herself and her obsessions. Five years after Hannah was born, Nina began to relapse, and her husband, Eric, prayed for a miracle. Soon their son, Christopher, was conceived. Today Nina is mostly recovered and remains in therapy, to stay one step ahead of her demons. She continues to grow in her relationship with God, and she and her husband are active in their church.

As I stared at those photos of Nina in 1997, something behind her eyes convicted me. She was choosing to live. Nina's story had a happy ending in process, because of the choices she was making.

And I knew eventually I, too, would have to choose.

And the Beat Goes On

*T*here comes a moment when we're faced with what we know to be true about God and what He says to be true about us, and we have to decide how we will act on that knowledge. I can say all day long that God loves me, but until I begin to behave in a way that aligns itself with that profession, I am nothing more than a poser.

There was no defining moment for me. I stayed sick a while longer, maybe another two years. I refused to go back into therapy, in part because I was in debt up to my eyeballs from inpatient treatment, in part because I was proud, and in part because I was tired of the whole scene. I didn't want to be anyone's "case" anymore. And realizing that, I think, was a significant step toward getting better.

Without making a conscious, pinpointed decision or announcement, I decided to try again at life. It must have been a gradual, cumulative sort of decision, because I don't remember it happening, only that it happened.

I joined a church and began singing and leading worship. Sometimes after church on Sundays, I would go to brunch. And eat.

I started working with the youth group. Sometimes during Thursday night meetings, we would order pizza. And I'd have some.

I met a cute guy in band rehearsals. Sometimes after practice, we would go grab a burger. And I'd share it with him.

Life began to happen, and I began to let it. It became more desirable to me, in most moments, than death. There were horrifying moments when I would go to get dressed in the morning, try on my size one jeans, then my size twos, then my fours—and they would not fit. When I couldn't button them, I would cry. At times I would cut or burn myself. I did this for a season, and I have a few scars as reminders. Each time I would listen to the voice, which would tell me to starve, call me a fat loser, try to persuade me to gobble down every pill in the house. But each time I did *not* do what she demanded, her voice grew weaker.

Don't misunderstand; it was a tumultuous time. I was torn between life and death, and such indecision cannot be anything other than maddening. There is a scene in the movie *Footloose*, where Ariel, the "wild child" main character, balances precariously on two cars as they speed down the highway, one foot in each car. As the cars veer away from one another, her legs spread further and further, until she is doing the splits and risking her life. Like Ariel, I had one foot still in death and disorder, but I had taken a leap out with the other foot and was doing the splits between two worlds. One would eventually have to win me over, or I would rend clear down the middle. Someone, just like in the movie, would have to snatch me into the car.

Someone did, and I married him. Hastily.

John was twenty-six, extremely handsome, a college graduate, and a Christian. More importantly, he was there. I was a twenty-three-year-old caught in a valley of indecision between life and death and figured maybe marriage was all I needed to push me over the edge and force me to choose. And John told me I was pretty. I desperately needed to feel pretty.

Both of us agreed, being twenty-three and twenty-six, that we were marriage-minded. Our pastor suggested we begin pre-marital counseling as soon as possible. One problem: I don't think either of us was sure, at that point, that we wanted to marry *each other*.

A sloppy, rushed courtship ensued, and John and I were married inside of a year. Looking back, of course, I realize this was a mistake. Life is not meant to move at the speed of light, and marriage is not meant to be a Band-Aid for a gaping wound. But nevertheless, I went from giggling girl to blushing bride that year, and within weeks, I went from newlywed to mother-to-be.

Now here was a switch. I knew with pregnancy my lifelong fears stood a good chance of coming true. Women gain weight during pregnancy—and some gain quite a bit. Every woman's body is different, from what I understand, as is every pregnancy. Thunder thighs and a jiggly belly could have been in my future at that moment, and the most bizarre phenomenon took place: I was overjoyed.

The months wore on, and while my marriage deteriorated and I got sick with pneumonia and my husband got fired from job after job and I worked long hours at a sales career I hated while stopping once in a while to throw up in the employee bathroom, I was ecstatic with glee. And why? Because my body—this ever-expanding, itching, stretching, heavy, round, swollen body of mine—was suddenly a great pleasure to me. The same body I had hated and despaired of and punished and starved and cut and burned and cursed for years was now doing me the ultimate favor, by fostering life and turning me into something I had always wanted to be: someone's mom.

I *loved* being pregnant. I felt beautiful for the first time in my life, and part of me wished I could stay pregnant forever. I found that, in some ways, pregnancy accomplished what I had relied on anorexia to accomplish. With my skeletal body, I had hoped others would see me as fragile and delicate, someone to handle with care. With my pregnant body, suddenly I was all of those things. There were other, less selfish reasons for my enjoyment of the pregnancy, like the sheer amazement I felt at each little kick, each tumble roll inside my womb, each inch larger I grew, knowing God was in action, creating a life, knitting together a human being, and I actually got to be a part of it.

I was sad when the pregnancy ended, but I got a wonderful consolation prize—one who cried and nursed and spit up and messed his diapers and looked like me, with a head full of reddish hair and a dimple on his left cheek so deep it looked as if it could collect water. I took him home and named him Jaden, which is a Hebrew name meaning "God hears us."

God had heard me, all those years. Every time I cried and screamed and begged Him to let me die, to send me a heart attack while I ran up and down the stairs ninety times in an hour. God had heard me every time I accused Him of creating a flawed, disgusting, inadequate, imperfect shell for me to inhabit. He had heard me call myself ugly and fat and stupid and worthless and guilty and shameful and punishable by death. He heard me and said only, "But I love you."

I did not understand this then. I only scarcely understand it now. But becoming a parent has lifted a corner of my blindfold and let me glimpse what God's love looks like. My son, Jaden, is incapable of doing anything—anything at all—that could make me stop loving him. There is nothing he could say or do, or forget to say or not do, that would ever diminish the love I have for him in my heart. He can't out-sin my love, just as I cannot out-sin God's love. I wish I had understood this better all those years ago. How different my first thirty-two years of life might have been if I had reached a better understanding of the value I hold in the eyes of God.

My former therapist Kris used to tell me, "Jena, the question cannot be *why*. 'Why' doesn't get us anywhere. 'Why' doesn't move us forward. The question you need to ask is, 'Now what?'" Writing a book was part of my answer. Writing a book about my recovery from an eating disorder would mean, to me and anyone else who labors under a performance mentality, that I had arrived. *Ta-da!*

But there was a fly in the ointment. Let's resume the story in July 2008, flip on the film projector, and watch. I had been doing rather well the past year or so, soldiering on against the disordered thoughts as they presented themselves and keeping the thoughts from turning into behaviors. With the aid of a counselor whom I adore, I had been diligently working to confront my lingering body image problems, and only a month before I'd seemed to be making "real progress."

Then I went to the doctor.

She weighed me.

Fade to black.

———

Okay, not quite. Almost.

I went to the doctor—Cathy, the nurse-midwife who delivered my son, actually—to get checked out for some unusual symptoms I had been experiencing. She examined me. She ordered blood work. Remembering me from when I was her high-risk mom-to-be patient six years before, she asked, "Do we still need to weigh you backward, or are those days behind you?"

"Goodness, no," I said with a flippant wave of my hand. "That was ages ago."

"Glad to hear it," she said with a nod. "All right, then climb aboard the old scale here."

I braced myself. I felt my heart skip a beat. My hands were sweating, and I clenched them into tight fists as I awaited the verdict: fat or not fat?

"Okay," Cathy said, sliding the metal weights across the bar. "And you are . . . 131 pounds, my dear."

Cathy said "131 pounds" as if this were a good thing. She smiled. Her words nearly made my ears bleed. I felt as if I could faint. My six-year-old sat quietly in the guest chair beside the exam table, coloring in his coloring book. She may as well have said, "And you are inadequate, my dear. You are a failure. You are hereby ordered to cease and desist from all eating, from this afternoon forward."

I am five-feet-six-inches tall, and a weight of 131 pounds is not overweight. I knew this even as Cathy was speaking the number, so I can't say why hearing the number spoken stirred such a reaction. Maybe it was simply the shock of being confronted with the fact, after seven years of utter denial, that I still *had* a body and therefore had a body weight. I had attempted to forget these facts by refusing to weigh myself and not having a scale in the house.

Whatever the reason, finding out what I weighed seemed instantly to release the chains on my old eating disorder demons. As they swarmed into my mind, pulled the blindfold over my eyes and taped my mouth shut, I thought, *Not again.*

The next day was Wednesday, and I had an afternoon appointment with the aforementioned counselor, Kris—who carries off the endearing dichotomy of soft blue eyes and sharp silver tongue. I told her about the doctor visit, explaining how much I regretted not allowing Cathy to weigh me backward. "I was trying to look normal and functional; it would have been embarrassing to admit I still struggle. I mean, someone could look right at me, weighing what I weigh now, and say, 'Really? You certainly don't *look* sick. Why on earth should I weigh you backward?' Anyway, so now I know what I weigh."

"Okay," Kris said, shifting in her chair, "and how are you doing with knowing your weight?"

"Not good," I admitted. "I don't know how normal people go about their day, knowing what they weigh and, um, eating anyway."

Kris laughed her wonderful rapid-fire machine gun laugh. "Well," she said, "normal people—and I dare you to show me a normal person, by the way—'normal' people don't let their weight define them. They keep it in the back of their minds, maybe, to ensure they don't consume an extra five hundred calories at each meal, but they are not consumed by it."

"I've been completely consumed by it ever since I heard the number yesterday."

"But you are still going about your day. You're not collapsing, which is good. You're eating . . ." She looked at me sideways, her open palms out in front of her, searching my face for clues. "You *are* eating, right?" she asked.

"Well, I haven't broken the fast just yet."

"You've been fasting?"

"I didn't set out to fast intentionally," I said defensively. "But I haven't eaten since before the appointment yesterday. It's not that big a deal."

"But it is, Jena. It is a big deal for you."

I looked at Kris like a kid who has been caught with something.

She said firmly, "You're to e-mail me after you eat dinner tonight."

I said I would. I didn't. I didn't eat dinner, certain that she would forget. Surely once I was out of her office, I wouldn't cross her mind again. Right?

At a quarter after nine the next morning, I got a call on my cell phone. The number didn't register on caller ID.

"How was dinner last night?"

I laughed, not knowing how else to respond.

"You did eat last night, right? I'm sure you just *forgot* to e-mail me," Kris probed.

I sighed. "I'll get back on track today."

"Wrong answer," she said. "What time do you leave for work?"

"Fifteen minutes from now."

"Do you have cereal in the house?"

I laughed again, because I was nervous and because I was in shock that someone cared this much. "Yes, I have cereal."

"Okay. I want you to take a few minutes and go eat a bowl of cereal."

I made an exasperated noise. I did not answer.

"It is *not okay* for you not to eat right now. There are people who love you, and we want you to be well. There are a whole slew of us who care about you and want you to be healthy. So go pour yourself some cereal. Right now."

"Yes, Mom." I sighed jokingly.

"And call me on your way to work."

"Are you serious?" I asked in disbelief. This was entirely beyond her call of duty, and I was both taken aback and deeply touched.

"I'm totally serious," Kris said firmly. "Call me back."

I forced myself to eat a quarter cup of cereal with skim milk and dutifully called Kris as I drove to work.

"I'm not trying to drive you crazy, Jena, and I'm not trying to be a bully," she said over the phone. "I am grabbing you back from the edge of the cliff so you don't fall over. You don't want that; I know you don't."

She was right. I didn't want to slip backward into harm's way; I didn't want to be less than a 100 percent mother to Jaden. These convictions had been solidified in my gut. But the evil thoughts rising up like a vile belch were not coming from my spirit. They were coming from the darkest corners of my mind, the recesses that had been only broom-swept and apparently never fully disinfected.

I saw Kris a week later. She asked me to go and get a physical. She asked me to sign a release of information authorizing her to speak with my physician regarding my health. She gave me a suggested food plan to follow, as if I hadn't had enough hours of nutrition didactics over the years to make me eligible for an honorary degree in dietetics. Knowledge, of course, does not always lead to action.

She covered all her bases and finally addressed the elephant in the room. "So," she said, her voice cracking, "you've already lost a lot of weight."

"Not a lot," I objected.

Kris looked away a moment, chuckled, then looked at me pointedly. "Have you weighed yourself?"

"Yes."

"I can *see* it, though," she said, not convinced. "That's disturbing: I can see it already, and it's only been a week. And because you know I care about you, this is concerning to me. I don't—and this is not a threat, it's a fact—I don't want to see you back in the hospital."

"I can't go back to the hospital," I interjected.

"Then you *have* to eat. There's no in-between. There's 'I

Hollow

eat: I don't end up in the hospital' or there's 'I don't eat, and I end up in the hospital or dead.' Those are your only options."

I didn't like hearing this. She was making it sound simple, and for me it had become anything but simple. She made it sound as if I knew what to do and was able to do it, and that was unnerving. It was especially unnerving because she was absolutely right.

———

Today this double-minded thinking remains a frustration: I know better—I've made the decision to live a life of relative wellness, to prioritize life and wholeness over sickness and disorder—and yet the temptation does not wane. If anything, I find myself needing to strengthen my resolve more and more as time goes by—as I age, as the average American grows steadily heavier, as I watch more and more girls succumb to the temptation to starve themselves to fit into an increasingly unrealistic mold.

The temptation is ongoing and palpable. I get angry when I catch myself longing for my sick, dysfunctional past. I wish I could say that it doesn't happen often, that I am 99 percent "over it"—that I have grown, blossomed, accepted myself, and healed.

This is far closer to the truth: I'm working on it.

A Work in Progress

My friend Jill has a little house in the woods not far from where I live. On several occasions God and I have used her house as a meeting place. Soon after I last relapsed, I made an appointment with God at Jill's house and later journaled about it:

I walk up to the charming little cottage, nestled in the woods and seemingly hidden from the world. Jill opens the door before I can knock and greets me with a sweet smile. "There's my Jena," she says, and I instantly want to cry—because she has called me "hers" and because she is an extension of the warmth and light and purity of Christ's love. As I approach her doorstep, I am suddenly aware of the darkness and filth that has attached itself to me in recent weeks.

I intentionally conjure up a mental image of myself dropping a dirty garment on the front porch as I step into her home, preparing myself to let go of any and all encumbrances that would keep me from what God has in store for me during my time of fellowship and reconnection with Him.

I sit on the stairs to greet Jill's fourteen-year-old bichon ever so carefully; she is easily overstimulated and will leave a puddle on the floor if she gets too excited. In a minute, she waddles away, arthritic, like a little old lady off to her afternoon nap. Jill pulls me into a hug and I overcome the knee-jerk reaction tendency to stiffen against her affection. I want her affection; I want her to hold me and stroke my hair and tell me everything is going to be all right. Truth be told, I want her to hug me and never let go.

But she cannot do that. Not only would it be inappropriate and absurd, but it would be insufficient. Jill is not my savior. She is wonderful at being Jill but surely not capable of being Jesus. But she is obviously a channel and a conduit of the love of Jesus, creating an environment where I can enter into the presence of God and experience the love and comfort that can only be found in the person of Christ.

On this particular day, I find that love and comfort. Jill provides a tranquil room with a lovely antique piano, recently restored and tuned. I pray. I read and meditate on "My Heart, Christ's Home." I journal. I sit at that piano for a solid hour and let my fingers do the worshiping.

About thirty minutes before I left Jill's house that day, I wrote these words:

You see my heart
and the darkness it holds;
You knew all its secrets
before they were told.
You hold it, embrace it
with no trace of disdain—
It's Yours, Your creation,
It's Yours to reclaim.
So take it, re-make it
what You meant it to be . . .
And I will be still
because You're holding me.

I'd enjoyed a sweet time of fellowship with the Lord, and I left Jill's house that day, went home, and had an argument with my mother on the phone, gave my son a time-out for saying a swear word, and found my sewer had backed up into the house and ruined my living room carpet. Stuff happens. My warm fuzzy "God feelings" don't last because they're only *feelings*.

Guilt is only a feeling. So are shame and fear and rage and hurt and anger. Feelings come and go. Acknowledging this has come as a great relief to me recently. Life, with all its drama, is fluid: it ebbs and flows and waxes and wanes and gets better and worse and horrible and awful and more bearable and wonderful and horrible again and then better. On a good day, life is beautiful. On a bad day, life is survivable. The trick is, simply, not to die.

I used to fear nothing more than giving up my eating disorder. I once thought that to grow in my faith and draw nearer to the heart of God, I would have to give it up first—100 percent of it. After all, the disorder is sinful, and God hates sin. I used to weep over the passage in Psalms that says, "Who may climb the mountain of the Lord? Who may stand in his holy place? Only those whose hands and hearts are pure" (Psalm 24:3–4 NLT). I felt condemned, believing these verses meant I could not struggle with an eating disorder and still come into God's presence. But I have discovered that, on the contrary, the only way to come to God is as I am, dragging whatever mucky barnacles have attached themselves to me. Only by bringing my filth before God would I ever have hope of being washed clean.

The eating disorder is not my identity, and it does not make me so ugly that God cannot bear to receive me. He can handle it. But He makes it clear that He does not want me to hold on to the disorder. He wants all of me—just like He wants all of you. He is not concerned with what I can or cannot do, what I have or do not have. He wants my heart, my love, my devotion, and my trust. He wants me to let go of all that would keep me from embracing Him fully. "But I *need* this," I tell Him. "No," He says gently, firmly. "You need Me and Me alone."

So how do I end a story that has not yet offered me an ending? Maybe I don't. After all, I'm still here, so my story hasn't ended. Life is a journey, so the cliché goes, not a destination. Maybe the victory doesn't reside in those two words *the end* as much as it speaks through the spaces *between* words, through the lives we lead when we think what we're doing doesn't matter. Maybe the victory is just in showing up for life, one day at a time, and learning and growing and discovering and exploring and messing up and saying "Sorry" and moving on and loving and living. Maybe the victory is in the living, and life is supposed to be messy sometimes—and that's okay.

So there shall be no ending. If you are the type of person who needs closure, I can leave you with this: My life is good. It's not perfect, but it's good. I might slip up again tomorrow, or I might be just fine. I could relapse in the future and wish I'd never written this book, but the plan is to keep on squeezing tightly to the hand of God and go on to focus my life and energy on other things.

Things far more interesting than eating disorders.

Can We Talk?

CHAPTER 27

I beg those of you who are struggling with your own disorder to believe life is worth living. I encourage you to let yourself off the hook, stop laboring under a false god's unrelenting commands, and grab the hand of God and hold on for dear life—and allow Him to hold on to you.

God wants you to experience His perfect peace. He wants you to be satisfied in Him. Isn't that a crazy thought? I spent many years refusing to believe that because it seemed in stark contrast to so much of what I had heard about God. But it's true. God delights in you, and He is most glorified in you when you are most satisfied in Him.

There are moments of happiness awaiting you, but beyond happiness, which is fleeting and circumstantial, God wants to give you "joy inexpressible and full of glory" (1 Peter 1:8 NASB). Joy is a fruit of the spirit, deep and real and abiding; it remains and sustains you even when your life falls apart.

Your life will fall apart, I assure you, at some point. We don't like to hear this—we who spend our days trying to manage our lives and everyone else's and keep all the balls in the air and make sure everyone keeps smiling—but we may as well accept it. People die and spouses cheat and children get sick and feelings get hurt and feathers get ruffled and hearts get broken. Life is messy, but it is worth sticking it out. Your story may look like a tragedy so far, but please, please, please stick around to see how it turns out. It's never too late to change your story.

You'll need help. You can't go it alone—period. Don't even try. You'll only wear yourself out. You'll disappoint and frustrate yourself, and eating disorders thrive on frustration and disappointment. You'll need an ally—at least one, preferably a Christian counselor with knowledge of eating disorders. Use discernment: not every therapist who prints a cross or a fish on her business card is a sound counselor. You might ask your church for a referral.

It is absolutely imperative to find someone with whom you can connect and eventually entrust with every secret. If, after a time, you don't feel you can trust a therapist enough to move forward, as I felt with Deb, whatever your reason, move on. When you find someone with whom you feel safe enough to work, then *work*. Commit to it, no matter what emotions it stirs. Let the feelings come. They're only emotions; they can't kill you.

It will be hard, it will be uncomfortable, and you may hate it. Don't quit. Your therapist may hit hot buttons you'd prefer to keep covered. Don't cancel that next appointment. In therapy, as in life, sometimes the victory lies in showing up.

If your illness has progressed, it's likely you have isolated yourself from the people who love you. I cannot stress this enough: stop it. People are meant to be interdependent. People need people. Isolation breeds all sorts of craziness in the sanest individuals. Especially with eating disorders, the surest way to lose the fight against your demons is to elope with them by isolating.

Whatever methods you choose, reach out. Keep praying. Journal. Stay positive. Dare to hope and dream and wonder and aspire. Play. Laugh. Forgive others and forgive yourself—daily. Become a friend of God. He wants to be your friend. He wants to give you a future and a hope. He is not mad at you. One more time: *God is not mad at you.* In fact, He is crazy about you.

I truly hope you make it. I've lost one too many friends to this illness already. We need more of us on the winning team. All it takes is a daily decision to choose life. Will you do that? Join the team. Bring others with you. While there is still time, change your story. Tell your story. I'd love to hear it.

If you don't know my friend Jesus, I'd love to introduce you. I don't know who you are or what belief system you subscribe to, but I respect you nonetheless. We all come from different backgrounds and upbringings and cultures. I love that about the world. We like to preach tolerance and quip that "we are all God's children." It's a lovely thought, but it is not true. We are all God's *creation*, yes. But we must *choose* to become *children* of God. Jesus is for everybody—Protestant, Catholic, Jew, Gentile, black, white, man, woman, rich, poor. You don't have to be perfect. You don't have to be holy or sinless or pristine. Jesus said, "*It is not the healthy* who need a doctor, *but the sick. I have not* come to call the righteous, *but* sinners" (Mark 2:17).

Are you one of us—one of the "sick"? Are you beat-up, burned-out on religion, jaded from life, and ready for something real? There is *nothing* more real than a relationship with Jesus Christ.

There is no magic prayer. You don't have to order a bottle of miracle water or pray on a bead or kiss a ring. You just have to come—as you are, right now. At my church, we use this prayer as a guide, so feel free to make it your own. It is your heart God hears, not any special combination of pre-written words. The power is not in the words, but in God's lavish grace and forgiveness in response to your desire to know Him.

Dear God, I believe that Jesus died for my sins and that He rose from the dead. I want personally to receive Your free gift of eternal life and forgiveness of my sins. With Your help, I am willing to turn from my sinful way of living. I give my life to You. Come into my life, and make me the kind of person You want me to be. From now on, You're the boss. Amen.

Choosing the Way

I had many reasons for writing this memoir, and none involved wanting to relive those painful years. Maybe I wanted to share my story in all its sordid, sorry detail with those who might consider anorexia glamorous and tempting—to expose the evil liar who whispers into the ears of young (and old) women (and men), promising contentment if they could just lose a few pounds.

Maybe I wrote it because, like it or not, my eating disorder is and was and has been part of me, and getting it down in print might get it *out of me,* lest it plague me forever. Maybe I wrote it because, as horrific as some of the memories are, my story includes a cast of characters who deserve to be given voice. Some have won their battles, tentatively but victoriously, while others have fallen victim, passing into tragically early graves. This is their story, too.

Often I struggled to find precise words to describe the indescribable. To this day, there are smells and settings that stir emotions and memories that simply cannot be verbally articulated. I could not find the words to describe how physically cold I was during my "lean years," nor could I accurately portray the palpable fear, the sense of dread, the hopelessness, the entrapment in my own mind.

I find it equally frustrating to convey my gratitude to God for sparing my life, for being so good and going so far to forgive my trespasses against my body, the temple of the Holy Spirit, and restoring it to foster life and bear a child. We serve a God of mercy and grace, and I understand both those words better for what He has delivered me from and forgiven me of.

Ask the eating disorder experts about the recovery rates for chronic eating disorders, and they will shrug and shake their heads. "It can be *managed* in some cases," they will say, "and that is the best one can hope for." Forgive my bravado and cockeyed optimism, but I disagree. I disagree despite the odds—despite the statistics, despite the growing dilemma of stick-thin fashion models and "pro-ana" websites, despite my own tendency toward a skewed body image and faulty eating habits.

I disagree because I *have* to. If I believe Jesus Christ was born, crucified, and rose so that I might have abundant life, I also have to acknowledge that abundant life—life "to the full"—leaves no room for anything so depleting and defeating as anorexia. God is not in the business of Band-Aid cures or empty promises. Though I'll be the first to admit His work in me has not yet reached completion; in this area or any other, I can confidently assert that the God I serve has not brought me this far to abandon me to my own devices. If He had, I would find myself in dire straits to be sure.

The fact is, I don't always want to work at it. There are days when I would rather return to destructive habits than lean on the everlasting arms of God, because the disordered habits would come so *naturally*. Fifteen years have passed since I was at my most ill, and still that surreal netherworld—my old stomping grounds of starvation—never feels that far behind me. It is still there, waiting for me with open claws. But what it has to offer is merely counterfeit for what I so desperately need, which is only found in my Savior.

I remember the day I sat with the art therapist at Chandler just before my final discharge papers were signed. She said, "You are going through a mourning period right now, because saying good-bye to anorexia is like saying good-bye to a friend who has been there for you. It helped you cope when you knew no other way."

But with revelation comes responsibility. Now I know another way to cope: I know, on a very personal level, the Way, the Truth, and the Life—and I have a responsibility to choose that Way, time and time and time again.

HUGE THANKS TO . . .

Mom and Dad, for teaching me much and loving me well, and for being good sports about this. I hope you both know how much I love you. None of us has walked an easy road, but we all made it.

My sister, Erica, for being one of my biggest fans in spite of my imperfections, none of which are hidden from you. I guess that's what this sister thing is all about. Few people "get me" like you do.

My son, Jaden, for showing me just how much I can love another human being. I think my heart stretches bigger each day because I just keep loving you more and more.

Laurie, for loving my dad as well as you do. I'm happy to call you family.

Pastor Clem and Anne Walchshauser, for so authentically practicing what you preach and for being there, always. I'm so privileged and blessed to do life with you. I am simply better off for knowing the two of you.

My extended family at Three Rivers Church, for being the hands and feet of Jesus in my life. I love serving with you, worshiping with you, and growing with you all.

Jill Fleagle, not only for writing the foreword to this book, but for your friendship, love, and prayer support. I could learn so much from you, and I'm honored that you've adopted me as your little sister.

Kris Walsh, for loving and accepting me in spite of all you know about me. You will probably never know all the ways God has used you to influence my heart and my journey. And all I can say is thanks.

Bonnie Schmitz, for years of valued friendship and for seeing my potential (and not resting until I began to see it myself). You continually challenge me to be a better writer and a better person.

Nicci Hejnar, for calling me a writer before I really felt like one and for always encouraging me to push beyond what I can imagine.

Nancy Langevin, for a sisterly bond that clearly withstands the test of time. I love you so much, and am grateful for the part you have played in my story and in my heart.

Wanda Draus and Millie Samuelson, for faithful prayer support and encour-agement at times when both have been crucial.

Heather King, for kicking me into gear and making me finish the manuscript in the first place.

Diana Flegal at Hartline Literary, for being one of the hardest-working agents in publishing, but also for being a dear sister in Christ, and such a source of encouragement, and for taking a chance on me.

Steve Lyon and the team at Moody, for patience, kindness, creativity, and trust.
You have made this fun, and I am honored and blessed to partner with you.

Ward and Kay Keller, founders of Remuda Ranch, for giving your lives to the cause of Christ through your wonderful, life-giving ministry. There are so many of us whose lives are testimonies to the impact you are having.

Friends who served as early readers for this book, whose input meant so much to me. Thanks to all of you, for caring enough to take the time.

Finally, thanks to my God, whose love for me is a "reckless raging fury," so deep and wide and tenacious and inexhaustible. Jesus, You are truly my all in all.

IF you are relatively normal, you probably wake up in the morning, switch on the coffee pot, pour some cereal, sit down with the morning paper, and eat your breakfast. You don't just stare at it; you eat it.

If you are me, or one of millions like me, your day looks a bit different. The food is not eaten casually or carelessly or even comfortably. Rather it is weighed, measured, agonized over, feared, loved, hated, resented, desired.

But this is life as you know it, if you have an eating disorder.

Meet Jena Morrow—singer, writer, mother of one, child of God … and recovering anorexic.

Jena wrote *Hollow* for anyone who battles this disease of the mind—or loves someone who does. It's an honest story of hope and healing, though Jena herself admits she's still a work in progress.

Hollow is an invitation to join her on the road to freedom: "I have discovered that the only way to come to God is as I am. Only by bringing my filth before God would I ever have hope of being washed clean." Are you filthy? Hollow? Guess what? So is Jena. But she's winning the battle—and so can you.

"If you or a loved one needs to know there really is a way out of the strong clutches of the self-hatred of an eating disorder, you will want to walk with Jena through each page. You will find a new strength and a fresh hope."
— **Gregory L. Jantz, PhD, C.E.D.S.**, founder, The Center, Inc.

"*Hollow* pulled me into a world I knew little about, held me there with its raw authenticity, and gave me empathy for those who struggle with eating disorders. Anyone battling food issues should read this. But more than that, anyone who loves someone in an eating disorder's clutches should read it."
— author of *Thin Places, a Memoir*

"Too often we want a happy ending. In *Hollow: An Unpolished Tale*, new author Jena Morrow treats us to an uncommonly honest portrayal of the recovery journey, and makes a hope-filled case for facing our fears, embracing our anger, and surrendering to the only One who can calm the storm within—even if (and when) it continues to rage."
— **Constance Rhodes**, founder, FINDINGbalance, Cofounder, The True Campaign

Learn more about JENA MORROW at **jenamorrow.blogspot.com**
Join the conversation at **hollowthebook.ning.com**

CHRISTIAN LIVING / PRACTICAL LIFE / WOMEN
ISBN-13 : 978-0-8024-4871-2
ISBN-10 : 0-8024-4871-2

$12.99

MOODY
PUBLISHERS

THE NAME YOU CAN TRUST®